Have ...*to Grieve?*

The sense of loss that accompanies the death of a loved one, the failure of a marriage or relationship, the termination of a job, or even the squandering of opportunities or talents is known, for lack of a better term, as *grief*. Ever since Adam and Eve were shown the way out of the garden, there is only one way to survive grief and that is to go through it, with Jesus Christ.

Noted Christian author Carol L. Fitzpatrick describes not only the stages of grief but shares poignant examples from her own life and from the Bible on how to deal with this devastating emotion. Always her focus is on the rough-hewn cross of Calvary, and the ultimate sacrifice of all time that purchased eternal peace.

Learn how to rid yourself of the grief-filled baggage of years past, and go on to lead the life God designed for you, a life filled with purpose. *It's time well spent.*

"After reading *A Time to Grieve* and studying His Word, you will be able to lift the heavy covering of grief. . .you will have the tools to find freedom and peace. Joy does come in the morning!"

Emilie Barnes
Author, speaker, and founder
of More Hours in My Day

A TIME TO GRIEVE

How to Get a *Grip* and Move On

Carol L. Fitzpatrick

A BARBOUR BOOK

Scripture quotations are taken from the New American
Standard Bible, unless otherwise stated, © 1960, 1962,
1963, 1968, 1971, 1972, 1973, 1975, 1977 by The
Lockman Foundation. Used by permission.

Published by   Barbour and Company, Inc.
                 P.O. Box 719
                 Uhrichsville, Ohio 44683

ISBN 1-55748-645-X

Printed in the United States of America.

Acknowledgments

God has sent many people to me who have generously shared their unique gifts. Those who have known Him have given their unconditional love and understanding. Among them was my grandmother, Mildred Pauline Merritt Hirsch, who always knew where I hurt and how to fix it. She taught me to pray.

Others who haven't claimed Jesus as their Savior visited on my life the grief of their own unresolved pain. However, God used even these hurtful times to rescue and enable me to draw near to His heart.

I am most grateful for both the *written* and the *living* Word of God, Jesus Christ, my Savior. Without these inestimable gifts I would have known neither *wholeness* nor *hope*.

Contents

1

Jesus' Own Bundle of Grief

Jesus wept. (John 11:35)

Grief sometimes approaches with gentle fingers of warning, as when one watches an older person come to the gradual close of his or her life. At other times grief overwhelms us with its sudden and shocking grasp. Yet it touches each of our lives with the same surety as tomorrow's sunrise. Grief is the process a person goes through when presented with a loss. And it can feel as real as a gaping wound.

If you're now working through grief, how are you coping? Perhaps you're courageously carrying on, reeling from the immensity of the event, but continuing to function as though your life hasn't been forever altered. You've managed to throw your best clothes on that beast called grief, and he doesn't look half bad. In fact, you might consider him presentable enough to incorporate into your daily routine. But what happens after you've tossed this hitchhiker in the corner of the bedroom at night and turned out the lights? There he sits, lurking in the shadows, glaring with those intense eyes, the ones that rob your soul of peace.

Maybe you've grown so weary of grief's grotesque face that you've covered it with the subtlety of withdrawal or the dark veil of destructive behavior. And still he haunts you, threatening to drag you over the edge of the cliff with him.

Is your method of coping working? Or does the silent ache within you call out for someone to trust? Can't anyone heal your pain?

The answer is emphatically yes! But you must be willing to release your burden slowly and surely, the same way you would excuse an unwelcome relative who has overstayed his or her welcome. Maybe, just maybe, you're ready at least to admit that grief is hiding, like a sleeping bag crammed deep into a stuff bag for storage.

One day a young woman named Lynn loosened the string on her own pouched bag ever so slightly as she walked into the office of a grief counselor. "I can't cry," she stated matter-of-factly.

"I see, and how long have you been experiencing this?" asked the therapist, a kind-looking woman in her early fifties.

"I guess it's about ten years now," Lynn answered flatly, as she brushed a light brown curl from the edge of her face.

"Do you want to cry?"

"Sometimes," she said.

"If you could release your tears, what would you cry about?"

"I don't know. I just think I need to, because I always have a knot in my stomach. My children cry and sometimes I want to join them."

"You said this problem started about ten years ago. Can you remember what happened then?"

A TIME TO GRIEVE

"My father died," she responded without displaying emotion.

"I see. And did this make you feel sad?"

"It was a shock. I was nineteen and when I came home from an evening of Christmas shopping, a neighbor was at our house. She told me, all in one quick sentence, that my father had died of a heart attack and I wasn't to cry and upset my brothers and sisters."

"Yes, and what did you do?"

"I choked back the tears and tried to help the younger kids."

"Did you ever allow yourself to grieve over your father's death?"

"No. . .I just tried to get on with my life."

After months of counseling, Lynn was gradually able to release her grief. But her pattern of detaching her feelings from accompanying events had started much earlier than ten years ago. She had systematically buried her emotions all her life. As each incident was finally confronted, the list looked like this: years of abuse in an alcoholic home; her father's early death, without either admitting his guilt or attempting to reconcile the fractured relationships in their home; the stillborn birth of her first child; and the stress of having three more children, each only a year apart.

But the worst deficit Lynn experienced was her lack of faith in her Creator. She neither understood His character nor His methods of molding her life to make her more like Jesus Christ.

Unfortunately, her problems are more typical than unique. Most of us have no idea how to work through an emotion as wrenching as grief. Lynn's breakthrough didn't occur until she ultimately got in touch with the One who knew her best, Jesus. In looking at His life, we can find a pattern for our own grief.

Do you remember when Jesus' good friend died? According to John 11:1-45, Jesus *purposely* delayed coming to be with Lazarus. By the time Jesus did arrive in Bethany, Lazarus had been dead for four days. He had already been buried. When Lazarus' sister Martha heard that Jesus had arrived, she went immediately to meet him. Martha does not mince words: If Jesus had been there *on time*, her brother wouldn't have died.

Let's look for a moment at why Jesus delayed coming to save Lazarus before he died. Was it a lack of love?

In verse 3, when the disciples tell Jesus that Lazarus is sick they say, "He whom You love is sick." Jesus' love for this family was perceived by those around Him. In fact, verse 5 confirms this strong bond: "Now Jesus loved Martha, and her sister, and Lazarus."

Therefore, is it possible that the delay actually has a greater purpose? In verse 4 Jesus says, "This sickness is not unto death but for the glory of God. . ." Jesus desired to use this incident to increase Martha's faith; God's awesome power was about to be demonstrated in a unique way. The full effect of this incredible miracle was dependent on Jesus' timing.

It's interesting that the disciples weren't concerned about the delay. "Rabbi, the Jews were just now seeking to stone You, and are You going there again?" (verse 8) *Jesus risked his own life to go back to Bethany and save Lazarus.*

Martha displays a small glimmer of faith in verse 22: "Even now I know that whatever You ask of God, God will give You." Then Jesus assures her that Lazarus will rise again. Martha knows that; she already believes in the Resurrection at the last day. But in verses 25 and 26 Jesus deepens her faith by saying, "I am the resurrection and the life; he who believes in Me will live, shall live even if he dies, and everyone who lives in Me shall never die."

Each of us must stop to answer the same question that Jesus then asked Martha: "Do you believe this?" In verse 27 Martha answers, "Yes, Lord,. . .I have believed that You are the Christ, the Son of God, *even* he who comes into the world."

Once Jesus has managed to bring Martha's heart to a point where she makes a statement of faith, she then goes to tell her sister Mary that Jesus is there. And what does Mary do? She starts the accusations all over again. "Lord, if You had been here, my brother would not have died," and she begins to cry. Can you see why the Bible tells us that Jesus ". . .was deeply moved in spirit, and was troubled?"

The point of this story is found in verse 35: "Jesus wept." (The word *wept* was taken from the Greek word *dakruo* which means "to shed tears.") Note that Jesus did not weep as the people around Him wept. Instead He *shed tears*. While they wept with loud crying and wailing, Jesus, on the other hand, knew that this was not the end for Lazarus.

Jesus shed tears for three reasons. First, He empathized with the relatives' and friends' loss and He understood the intensity of their sorrow. Second, His tears represented an acknowledgment of their present state of unbelief. Jesus had finally managed to help Martha's faith to move forward, but now her sister Mary is back at square one!

But Jesus shed tears for a *third* reason, and that was to let the world know that grief *is* an appropriate emotional response to pain and loss. He didn't stuff his emotions into a hidden compartment or wait for an appointed time of grieving. He allowed Himself to feel the intensity of

His pain *at the time it occurred.* Jesus didn't stifle His agony or extinguish the feelings. Instead, He allowed His sadness to show.

The unhealthy alternative to Jesus' example is to wait for the inevitable surfacing of these feelings of grief within some destructive behavior. Such postponement of grieving damages and consumes not only ourselves but everyone close to us. Yet before we can discuss the *benefits of grieving,* we need to present a *process for grieving.* If Lynn, whom we discussed earlier, had understood her full range of emotions, she would have recognized that one as important as grief could not be ignored. Attempting to hide her true responses had resulted in detachment. The full impact of her self-made prison came as she watched her children release their own tears.

Initially, Lynn had to *localize her pain.* When the therapist asked her what had happened ten years earlier, she immediately responded, even though she hadn't worked through the resulting problems. For other people the initial source of pain may not be as obvious. Lynn's therapist routinely encouraged her patients to keep a journal. She knew that as they continued to write about their pain, they would eventually come to understand it. As Lynn recorded different incidents, a pattern emerged. She had no labels to describe her emotions, even the happy ones. She had settled for living on a *vanilla plane,* "numbing out" most of the time. When upset, she rarely understood why and in nearly every instance the degree of anger she felt had nothing to do with the actual incident that seemed to trigger its release.

What finally surfaced was the fact that the home in which she had been raised had been extremely traumatic. Her father was an alcoholic who vacillated between abuse and doting. When he drank he lashed out at his children with verbal, physical, and sexual abuse. And when he was sober, his family saw glimpses of his basically fun-loving personality and natural teaching capabilities. To survive this precarious existence, Lynn repressed everything she experienced.

The harmful memories were shoved down into her stuff bag; she couldn't function if she dwelled on them. Positive memories were perceived either as undeserved or unreliable. They could be taken away on a whim by the father whom she expected to cherish her. But he didn't know how to love her.

A radio interview conducted by Dr. James Dobson of Focus on the Family with Dave and Jan Dravecky demonstrates well the importance of hidden feelings.* The Draveckys were talking about their new book, *When You Can't Come Back* (Zondervan, 1992). Dave, a pitcher for the San Francisco Giants, had surgery for cancer in his pitching arm and then came back to lead the Giants to an emotional major league victory. Five days later, while pitching his second game, Dave's arm broke with a resounding crack, and a short time later had to be amputated. On the air Dave and Jan related their grief process. Shortly before this incident both of Jan's parents had died. She hastily buried those first distressing emotions and by the time she and Dave began to undergo this new tragedy, extreme depression threatened to overtake her. Although he didn't realize it at that time, Dave also needed to grieve: for the career that was taken from him and the consequent feelings of loss.

Despite the Draveckys' initial idea that Christian coun-

---

* Interview aired October 14, 1992, on "Focus on the Family" radio program.

seling was a sign of weak faith in the Lord, through solid biblical counseling and study of God's Word, Dave and Jan were able to identify their pain, spend time grieving, and start over with renewed strength.

God is ready to strengthen you, too, no matter what your source of grief or how long you have attached yourself to it. *Remember, God packs a special suitcase for us when He sends us on our journey to earth.* Inside He places knowledge of Himself, but He also fills it with all the talents and skills we're going to need in order to survive. But instead of looking inside the suitcase He's supplied and seeing those things, we proceed to stuff it full of such unnecessary items as grief, worry, pain, unforgiveness, anger, and repressed memories.

For those who might be wondering why you even picked up this book on grief in the first place, let's identify what many people are grieving about. While all of us should take time to grieve over the passing of friends and relatives, sometimes, even during funerals, people focus on inconsequential things to cover up or minimize their true concerns. After all, attending either a formal church ceremony or a memorial service is bound to be a blatant reminder of our own mortality.

This can be expressed loudly by the person who declares, "I *know* I'm going to be fifty, and I don't want a birthday party!" Or it can be more subtle, taking the same route of quiet depression as Jan Dravecky.

The end of a romance or a divorce are other sources of grief. Divorce in particular affects the entire family, especially when holidays and other special occasions are being celebrated and that estranged person no longer is included in family events. We may even grieve at a certain time of year when we are reminded of the loss of a loved one or relationship.

People consistently grieve over things beyond their control: losing a job, not getting promotions or opportunities, or the effects of natural disasters. Some grown individuals are still grieving for the childhood they lost when suffering some kind of abuse, and they find it necessary to begin self-parenting for their own survival.

It becomes imperative to treat the *string of events* that comprises the whole of a person's grief. Think for a moment about those link sausages you can buy in a meat market. Sometimes our grief is like that: The death experience may be connected to many other unresolved issues. One of the reasons Lynn buried the grief from her father's untimely death was because her own daughter's death became connected to those years of growing up in an alcoholic and dysfunctional home. She couldn't deal with those deaths because she had stuffed the feelings they were connected to way down into that suitcase she had repacked for the Lord.

Realistically, while on earth all of us can expect to encounter death and suffering. The Bible says, "Then *comes* the end, when He [Christ] delivers up the kingdom to the God and Father, when He has abolished all rule and all authority and power. For He must reign until He has put all His enemies under His feet."(1 Corinthians 15: 24-25) Yet verse 26 is the most important: "The last enemy that will be abolished is death." On the cross Jesus defeated sin and death so that all believers could go to heaven when they die. However, Satan's reign of evil will not be over until the final days.

Suffering is also a cause of grief, but we should be prepared for it. First Peter 4:12, 13 says, "Beloved, do not be surprised at the fiery ordeal among you, which comes upon you for your testing, as though some strange thing were happening to you; but to the degree that you share the sufferings of Christ, keep on rejoicing; so that also at the revelation of His glory, you may rejoice with exultation."

Can you see how important it is to find a meaningful way to grieve? When we learn to *trust God's judgment, rely on His strength*, and *continue in our walk,* life's circumstances will not paralyze us.

Let's return to Lazarus in order to apply the reasons for Christ's delay to the times the Lord seems to wait on answering requests in our own lives. Christ's delay was purposeful and done out of love not only for Lazarus but also his family. Second, it was for the glory of God. Had Jesus not waited until everyone was absolutely positive that Lazarus was dead, there would always be that little doubt as to just how big a miracle He had actually performed.

Third, it was part of God's complete plan for Lazarus, just as He has an itinerary for each of us. "All the days ordained for me were written in your book before one of them came to be." (Psalm 139:16, NIV) We can thus look beyond the individual purpose God has for our lives, and look more studiously at God's Word. All sixty-six books of the Bible work together to help us understand how God's overall plan for humankind has always been accomplished.

From the story of Lazarus we know that Jesus' *timing* for answering is *perfect*. Just as He did for Lazarus, when the timing is right, He will apply the very power of His Resurrection to both our problems and our lives.

The fifth lesson to be understood is that the delay is to deepen our faith in His power. Martha went from a small seed of faith to understanding the real Jesus who stood before her, both God and man.

Jesus is willing to take a risk on us, too. In the same

way He risked His life to bring life to Lazarus, He has already given His life for us.

Before you read any further, perhaps this is a good place to answer life's most important question. What have you done about Christ's dying for you? Do you comprehend the significance of His sacrificial act? Have you surrendered your life to Him, so that He can now apply His Resurrection power to your life? *Jesus is the Resurrection and the Life.*

Only Jesus can enable you to get beyond grief and into really living your life. Most important, He's willing to take you, just as you are. As we cry out in our despair and pain, God hears us. Martha and Mary *longed for Christ's presence.* This was evidenced by the opinion they knew and voiced, that just His appearance would have an effect on the final outcome for their brother. Do you long for Christ's involvement in your life? Do you seek solace in His Word?

Martha and Mary eventually understood that the very delay, which was so frustrating to them, actually allowed God to perform a more extravagant miracle in their lives. Can you also relinquish control of timing and circumstances to a God who is powerful enough to raise the dead?

Martha and Mary placed their trust in Jesus. Is your grief greater than theirs? The end result to them was that Lazarus came forth to new life. Are you ready to allow the Lord to provide you with a new life? These two women finally understood God's exchange system. They released something impossible to bear—their grief—and He replaced it with *faith* that would be lived out in their own lives. Now they could be absolutely positive that because Jesus' power raised Lazarus from the dead, the Resurrection was a reality for them as well.

2

Suitcases for Stages of Grief

Precious in the sight of the Lord
is the death of His godly ones. (Psalm 116:15)

While we wrap ourselves in a wretched dark garment of grief over losing loved ones who died believing in Christ, God is clothing them in robes of righteousness. As we read and study the Bible, the truth of this teaching is revealed: "Therefore, being always of good courage, and knowing that while we are at home in the body we are absent from the Lord—for we walk by faith, not by sight—we are of good courage, I say, and prefer rather to be absent from the body and to be at home with the Lord." (2 Corinthians 5:6-8) Why, then, is our grief so intense, bitter, and all consuming?

Perhaps the best reason is that we don't understand how to let go of our pain in stages. Instead, we either try to deny the facts before us or we attempt to rush into the category of *full acceptance* before we even understand our needs. The bottom line is, we just don't want to *hurt through the process of healing*. Yet as an ordinary wound shows visible stages of mending, so also our soul requires cure time.

In the previous chapter we discussed Psalm 139 and found that God has appointed a time for us to die. From the moment we were conceived, that date has been fixed in time. But when those we love are called home years before their "allotted" life expectancy, our inborn sense of fairness cries foul. We aren't like household appliances that come with a limited warranty. *As human beings, we are part of God's plan.* And He makes the decision as to the length of that earthly lifespan.

A "20/20" television broadcast once featured interviews with people who lived to be 100 years and older.* These men and women had many things in common. First, they all had a strong faith in Christ and expressed this openly. They displayed a sweet and gentle spirit. None of them was driven by the passion to succeed or consumed with anger and vengeance. Also, they were optimistic about life and had a genuine love for other people.

Not surprisingly, each of them had suffered some type of loss in their lives but they had learned how to grieve in healthy ways. *All were hopeful about the future and saw a purpose for their lives.* These individuals were in touch not only with their own feelings, but those of others as well. Their lives continued to have an impact in this world.

A friend of mine, Rigo Lopez, began his journey through the stages of grief when he learned he had terminal cancer. Not easy news for a man in his early forties with two young children. At first he was in shock, hoping and praying for a miracle cure. One did not exist, however, for his type of melanoma.

Rigo's trek would have been easier if the stages of grief had been neatly marked out, like the yellow lines people draw on roadmaps as they plan a trip. But they weren't.

---

* Aired November 20, 1992.

In fact, sometimes these stages even begin overlapping each other.

As Rigo tried to release his grief, he became depressed while searching in vain for a support group with other terminal cancer patients. *However, when he armed himself with prayer that the Lord would enable him to face reality, he became convinced that he could initiate such a group himself.* Many who attended the weekly meetings were not Christians. They merely came in search of finding a purpose for the remainder of their time on earth. Through Rigo's obedience to the call the Lord had placed on his life, he was able to lead many of them to a commitment in Christ.

As I watched Rigo, allowing God to use all the physical and emotional strength he possessed, an idea surfaced for spreading the information he had learned about life, love, and grieving. During that time, when many would have chosen selfishly to hoard each moment for themselves, Rigo instead allowed me to write his testimony for *Decision* magazine.* While cancer ravaged his body, his mind remained focused on Christ. Rigo's message of hope went across the world in English, Spanish, and braille. Finally, as he'd progressed his way up the final stairs, marked *acceptance, adjustment,* and *interaction*, the Lord called him home to glory.

The ultimate gift that each of us can hope to give back to God is to allow Him to use our life in the way of His choosing, without reservation. Instead, many of us remain in the first of the five stages of grief, that of *shock or denial*. No matter how you look at it, denial is debilitating.

---

*Carol L. Fitzpatrick, "The Story of Rigo Lopez," *Decision* magazine, April 1987.

Rigo never relinquished his belief in God's capability to bestow a complete, if not instantaneous, healing on his body. On the other hand, he didn't waste critical moments having a pity party and asking, "Why me?" Instead, he used every day allotted to him. Rigo saw time as his irreplaceable and precious commodity.

How was he able to move forward rather than allow the weight of grief to cause him to withdraw and wither? The answer is, he *did* those things. These are normal reactions to the initial phase of grief. However, his *faith* was rooted in the *person*, Jesus Christ, not in a system that might fail him. Because of that, Rigo was able to get beyond those frustrating feelings. He understood God's character and steadfastly believed two things. He was convinced first that God's powerful strength, as described in Psalm 55:22, could hold him firmly: "Cast your burden upon the LORD, and He will sustain you; He will never allow the righteous to be shaken."

Secondly, Rigo believed in God's unshakable love for him. "I love those who love me; and those who diligently seek me will find me." (Proverbs 8:17) He had made a strong commitment to the Lord and his life had been transformed by God's power. Now it was time for him to understand fully that he shouldn't try to equate suffering with punishment.

The fact that Rigo's life was ravaged with cancer had nothing to do with whether or not God loved him. "For I am convinced that neither death, nor life, nor angels, nor principalities, nor things present, nor things to come, nor powers, nor height, nor depth, nor any other created thing, shall be able to separate us from the love of God, which is in Christ Jesus our Lord." (Romans 8:38, 39)

Rigo allowed God to have full rein and decision-making

power in his life. He was at peace because he had accepted God's will for his life, and not his own. Rather than internalize the pain, Rigo instead chose to trust the Lord's judgment and tenacity to get him through, *one day at a time.*

The next stage of grief is that of *relief or catharsis.* A woman named Sandra, whose father died when she was in her late twenties, has not yet progressed through this stage. Now in her mid-thirties, she still refers to her dad as a "street angel and a house devil." Evidently, he portrayed one face to those close to him and another to the world. Even after several years, Sandra can still recall the relief she experienced as he lay dying in a hospital. And as she approached his casket at the funeral, she remembers thinking, "Now you got just what you deserved and I'm glad you're dead."

When asked whether she can understand *why* she experienced such a sense of deliverance at her father's death, she is unable to cite specific details of abuse. Nevertheless, she displays some of the classic characteristics of a traumatized person: withdrawing if touched unexpectedly, being extremely sensitive to criticism, expressing total denial of issues, and having no real childhood memories. Situations that *are* remembered show marked detachment from normal grief responses.

Like Lynn, whom we discussed in the first chapter, only God's healing touch will enable Sandra to understand how she can reattach her feelings to her life experiences. Unaware, she has become entangled in this second stage of grief. The real danger of remaining stuck in any of the normal transitions of grief is that *true emotional growth might never take place.*

Therefore, it is important to *localize your pain.* Perhaps

in your past there are still painful and unresolved issues. Perhaps the only clue you may have to a problem is the fact that something is *illogical*, since sorrow is the response that the loss of a parent should evoke. So, start there. This will be discussed in more detail in another chapter.

The third stage of grief is *depression, anxiety, or guilt.* A certain amount of depression is to be expected in any grief-producing situation. However, if there are visible signs of complete withdrawal, inability to function in your normal environment, or deep hostility, then it's time to get help. When, for example, Jan Dravecky's depression became more than she could bear, she wisely enlisted the assistance of others. A qualified and recommended Christian counselor or a friend who has experienced a similar situation can be almost equally effective. Joan, a woman in my church who has a great capacity for listening, suffers from multiple sclerosis. She has a music ministry outreach, along with public speaking, in spite of the fact that she walks with the assistance of crutches. She teases that the Lord is welcome to use whatever is left of her for His work. Indeed, He pours her life out as a blessing to others. Joan has learned that her own suffering has produced the gift of compassion.

Another example is my maternal grandmother. Her own mother died of tuberculosis when she was only a baby. Although she grieved for the loss of that special relationship all her life, she also allowed the Lord to channel this feeling. In releasing her excruciating pain, she learned to reach out to others in the ways she so fervently wished her own mother could have expressed love to her. While she had always managed to convey that I was loved and special to her, it was not until her funeral that the entire family realized she had managed to accomplish this—one on one—with hundreds of others. She willingly surrendered her grief to Christ, and received, in turn, an incredible ability to communicate His love to others.

The opposite of these positive examples is the person who falls prey to *anxiety* and *guilt* during their crisis with grief. These feelings may be due to real situations that weren't appropriately concluded or forgiven before the death of a loved one. At other times these emotions may be due to *perceived* thoughts and hurts. Those who are suffering a loss may focus on themselves, God, or perhaps the tragedy itself. They may appear overly exhausted, unable to concentrate or make decisions, and could even experience physical symptoms. Therefore, it is critical that they begin to work through this time.

Another temptation when grief swiftly sideswipes our lives is to think that as Christians we should be immune from such suffering. Why? If Christ Himself experienced grief, then how can we even entertain such a thought?

It's perfectly normal to feel some guilt for things we could have said and didn't, for not loving enough, or not being kinder. After all, once a person is dead, we have lost our ability to affect their lives again. However, if people have an abnormal level of frustration connected with reality, then they must work hard at identifying their true source of pain. As supportive friends, we can refrain from offering pat answers to their expressed grief and spend time both listening and observing their needs. Don't run from their burdens, as it will only enable them to bury their discouragement deeper. This is an opportunity to discover together the mercies of the Lord.

When ministering to a loved one, of tremendous importance is not to lock him or her into a specific timetable for recovery. Most of us are able to endure someone's grief for a short period of time. Yet for each of us there is a specific amount of time required for our healing process, *however long it takes*. Allow those you care about to talk about their issues and be patient. This may be the first time they have been confronted with a crisis as overwhelming as grief. They have no plan for beginning to understand the pain. But along with freedom to express their true emotions will come a fresh desire to grow more positive beyond the devastation.

The fourth stage of grief is *facing reality*, and for many this may seem an insurmountable task. After all, the change they must endure may be a *completely altered life*. Take, for instance, the unprovoked physical attack of one young man named Brian.

As the tall, well-built night janitor of a large hospital, Brian would collect and dispose of daily hospital refuse. In the early hours of one fateful morning, he approached the large Dumpster and made ready to heave his heavy bundles into the metal container. Without warning he was hit on the back of the head and fell to the pavement. A brutal attack by two men wielding knives ensued as they attempted to rob him.

With Brian slumped into a sitting position, the men continued in vain to retrieve his wallet. Furious that Brian seemingly wouldn't cooperate, one of the men plunged a knife deep into the left side of his chest, and again a second time the weapon punctured his body. Now bleeding excessively, the young man attempted to stop the ruthlessness directed at him. Reaching out to grab his assailant, Brian asked, "Why?"

Finally fearing their imminent discovery, the two men fled the scene, leaving Brian to die in the pool of blood.

Knowing that if he didn't get immediate attention death would become reality, Brian determinedly rose to a semistanding position and staggered to the hospital's emergency room entrance. There he was met by a compassionate stranger standing in the doorway who removed his own shirt to apply pressure to Brian's gaping injury. This one act of kindness may have made the difference whether Brian lived or died. By the time hospital personnel began life-saving procedures, Brian had already lost three and a half pints of blood.

However, Brian's survival was only the first of his hurdles toward recovery. Such traumas as memory loss due to oxygen deprivation, bungled tests to evaluate the initial damage, and insensitivity of medical personnel became daily challenges. Now, a year after the attack, Brian suffers from continual cerebral seizures, has experienced loss of feeling in his left leg, walks with a brace, and is unable to work. Brian also has a daily pass on the emotional rollercoaster common to victims of violent crime.

An extremely gentle and forgiving person, Brian made a conscious decision before leaving the hospital that he would not allow this incident to make him into a bitter, resentful human being. Perhaps verbalizing this so soon after the attack might have caused some to doubt his sincerity. However, over the past year, he has consistently applied this loving attitude to those who seek to tear away at his self-esteem, integrity, and stamina. His character remains intact, in spite of this traumatic event.

How can we manage to maintain our personal integrity, despite great physical loss? *By believing that Christ is acting in our best interest, even though circumstances belie this reality.* While others shriek out in pain and seem to bend like willow trees in a storm, never managing to retrieve their faith in God's ability to keep them, we must allow tragedy to enable us to become a stronger people. Our endurance is not due to a denial of the facts, but rather a *belief in God's sovereignty.*

Perhaps one of the most famous figures from history who turned a tragedy into an opportunity was Scottish-born Alexander Graham Bell. Although a distinguished scientist, Bell is most recognized as the inventor of the telephone. Yet few may realize that this invention, as well as many others, was merely a by-product that grew out of Bell's deep need to communicate with both his deaf mother and his own deaf wife. In fact, the majority of Bell's life was dedicated to teaching the deaf and dumb.

God is not going to take away every trial you have. But He has promised to provide a way *through* the trials. In Psalm 16:11 (NIV) we find the way out: "You have made known to me the path of life; you will fill me with joy in your presence, with eternal pleasures at your right hand." God also has a purpose for your suffering, just as He does for mine.

Each year I spend some time thinking about the daughter I lost, a stillborn birth. The day I miss her the most is her birthday. Although I long to do something special with her, which I know is impossible, recently I wrote a poem for her (see page 33) and sent it to all my friends who have also lost children. No matter how much time has passed since the death of a child, we will always grieve for their presence. Hopefully, we will not experience debilitating grief but sadness, for what might have been.

Interestingly, most of the people discussed did not hold grudges against those who had harmed them or against God for allowing challenging circumstances to enter their lives. Nothing can stifle our growth like *an unforgiving heart.* Yet one of the reasons we don't want to forgive someone is because we think it somehow makes what they did to us right. *Nothing can make a wrong done to us right—either in our eyes or the Lord's—but that's not the purpose of forgiveness.* God uses forgiveness to *heal our own heart* and release our shackled spirit from bitterness and pain.

Ideally, when we *accept* the loss of those we love we become prepared to *face the reality* of our own deaths. If we firmly believe that we will be with Christ after death, then crossing the bridge to eternity does not have to be a dreaded event. Rather, we can anticipate this stage of life. We can prepare for our death as an inevitable journey that will take us back to God, and not view it as some morbid, horrible end. Grandma Slabach's departure was recorded as "Grandma's Great Adventure" in *Focus on the Family* magazine by her daughter-in-law Gertrude.* Grandma Slabach's incredible attitude enabled those who loved and surrounded her to see death not as a terrifying experience but as simply a natural closure. She not only expressed her own fears but also stated her faith. In addition, she admonished her family members, old and young alike, to cry and express their grief. She had managed to grasp the fact that as humans they needed to grieve but also to understand that she would be waiting for them in heaven.

Perhaps if we focus on what heaven is like we will be able to release some of our fears. First, *heaven is the place where God dwells.* Jesus said to the multitude, "I know Him; because I am from Him, and He sent Me." (John 7:29) He left the only *place of perfection*—because if God dwells there it is perfect—to come down here to

---

*Gertrude M. Slabach, "Grandma's Great Adventure," *Focus on the Family,* August 1993, pp. 6-7.

save us and also to assure us that now we are eligible to come there, too. That was Jesus' message to Martha and Mary, remember? He told them about the Resurrection.

Heaven is also a place in which our uniqueness as human beings will be preserved. After Christ had risen from the grave, He had a "fish fry" with His disciples on the beach. "Jesus said to them, 'Come *and* have breakfast.' None of the disciples ventured to question Him, 'Who are You?' knowing that it was the Lord." (John 21:12) The disciples knew and recognized Him, even though He appeared to them in His resurrected body. The same was true of Lazarus. He, too, manifested the same physically remembered characteristics as he had before his death. As Lazarus danced his way out of the funeral wrappings that bound him, those in attendance knew him once more. *We will be known in heaven by others.*

Of course, the most comforting thing about heaven is that our trip there will be immediate: As soon as we're dead, we arrive. When Christ Himself was dying on the cross, the thief hanging next to Him asked, "Jesus, remember me when You come in Your kingdom!" And Jesus said to him, "Truly I say to you, today you shall be with Me in Paradise." (Luke 23:43)

Without hesitation, Jesus issued assurance to the man that there was indeed a place for him in heaven. The reservation hinged on the man's belief in Jesus and acknowledgment of the sacrifice made in his behalf. For this guilty man hanging next to Christ, the perfect sacrificial lamb, paradise became a reality. Have you placed your hope in Jesus?

A TIME TO GRIEVE

A CHILD IN HIS GARDEN

He left the gate open
ever so slightly
Pushing it gently, I boldly peeked in
at flowers standing in full array
He knew once I saw it
I'd surely want to stay.
I walked down the path
that wound through the glade
Lush green tufts were home
to bunnies who played
Finding a small white bench
I sat and reflected.
'Til I felt the presence
of someone coming near
If this is your garden,
may I stay here a while?
He nodded while planting
a fragrant pink rose.
Your flowers are lovely
I'm glad that I came
Please tell me,
whatever is your name!

He looked deep into my eyes
as peace flooded through me.
Then I knew that it wasn't
a gardener sitting beside me
But the tenderest of souls
Wrapping protective arms
'Round my shoulders
He said I'd never grow old.

A TIME TO GRIEVE

No more will you wander
afraid and alone
A flower on loan,
my garden's fine treasure.
I missed you...
So I called you home.

3

Locating Your Luggage of Pain

And He shall wipe away every tear from their eyes;
and there shall no longer be any death;
there shall no longer be any mourning,
or crying, or pain;
the first things have passed away. (Revelation 21:4)

On the night He was betrayed Jesus once again went to
the Mount of Olives, ". . .as was His custom. . . ." (Luke
22:39) But on this occasion, the last time He would pray
in the garden, Jesus took His disciples with Him for comfort and support. He also requested that they raise their
supplications to the Father so that they would not enter
into temptation. Then He withdrew from them and began
His own prayers.

To those who had followed Him for three years this was
just another night with Jesus. Knowing the disciples misunderstood the importance of His admonition, Jesus en-
treated the Father, and "His sweat became like drops of
blood. . . ." (Luke 22:44) Those He had asked to support
Him faithfully in prayer had fallen asleep.

Have you ever experienced this kind of *abandonment*
during your own hour of need? Can you imagine how

Christ felt, knowing that those who had served with Him for so long still could not recognize the impact of His carefully chosen words? He asked the disciples to pray because He knew their faith was about to undergo its greatest test. Yet He understood that it was their sorrow that caused them to fall asleep. Even so, He gave them another chance, again asking them to pray.

But it was too late. The chief priests and officers of the temple, along with the elders, were already upon them. Now Peter would walk into one of the greatest crises of his life and he would be without the spiritual support necessary to sustain him. Jesus had expressed sorrow that none of them had taken time to prepare themselves. Now His grief would be not only for this moment, but also for the time when He would no longer be physically present on earth with them. Is it any wonder that the disciples had no strength for Christ's trial, crucifixion, and the events that followed?

Jesus had *localized his pain*. He had told the disciples exactly what He needed and they had failed Him. But that was only the first of the ways in which they had abandoned Him. Later most of them would run away. And Peter, who had sworn to love Him, would end up denying ne ever knew Christ, not once but three times. Only later when Jesus' eyes of love pierced through his soul would Peter remember that Jesus had tried to warn him.

Is your pain greater than that of Christ? Remember, Jesus *forgave* and acquiesced to start over with those same disciples. He understood their weak human condition; He knew they had not tried to hurt Him *intentionally*. Jesus knew that eventually these very weak vessels would go on to become deep men of faith, the anchors of His church.

Who in your life has trampled on your emotions or rudely

ignored your needs? Monica, a small, frail girl with long, dull-looking hair, approached the piano bench. Once again her teacher quickly became impatient and upset. Within moments the adult became so enraged at Monica's repeated mistakes that she slammed Monica's small, slender fingers into the ivory keys. "You're slow and stupid," shrieked her school-appointed music teacher. Monica bolted from the room in tears, never again in her youth to muster the confidence to play this or any other instrument.

Her instructor never bothered to invest time in understanding the reason Monica couldn't concentrate. The child came from a large, impoverished family where there was never enough food for a nourishing breakfast. In addition Monica suffered from a low blood sugar condition that made her especially susceptible to both loss of memory and concentration when she hadn't eaten enough protein.

Have you allowed a similar incident in your own past to cripple you and keep you from reaching your own dreams and expectations? For over thirty years Monica repressed this horrible memory until many years of counseling enabled her to understand her uniqueness in Christ, finally restoring her confidence.

As an adult, she has begun once again to experience wonderful and melodious sounds in her head. The Lord has truly revitalized the music she had heard as a child. Monica found an exceedingly patient piano teacher and started over. Now she writes down the lyrics and music that invade her sleep at night. She's finally begun to use her God-given talent.

The choice to allow the Lord to work through our grief is always ours. Since God gave us a free will, it's up to us to look to Him as each challenging situation in life is presented. He is waiting and ready for us to come to Him to exchange our turmoil for His insight, strength, and coping mechanisms.

A courageous woman, Marguerite has learned what it means to localize her pain. One evening she and her husband heard their daughter's car as its tires crunched across the leaves scattered at the end of their driveway. When after a few moments Laura Anne didn't enter the house, her parents went outside to look for her. The car door was flung open, but she was gone without a trace.

For three days the police searched for her and finally they located her body. The newspapers said she died of multiple gunshot wounds to the head and shoulders. Clutched inside her hand was a crucifix. Even as Laura was being pursued on a hilltop, so close to the town where she lived with her family, she prayed while two teenagers casually snuffed out her twenty-one-year life.

As the family planned the unexpected funeral, necessary activities crowded out the reality of this horror. Only after Laura's burial did Marguerite finally face the events that had taken place. She describes that time as "walking in the shadow of the cross and letting it hover over. . . , being fearful of looking up, as though this acknowledgment would bring its crushing weight shattering down."*

During this horrendous and wrenching time, Marguerite says she felt as though she were running. One day, however, the exhaustion from her race became too much and from the depths of her soul came a silent cry. "Jesus, You know I can't carry this cross—it's too immense! It's too final! I can't carry it—but it has to be carried—so

---

*Marguerite Stoughton, "Death of Our Daughter," *Leaves* magazine, Jan.-Feb. 1978, P.O. Box 87, Dearborn, MI 48121, pp. 6-7. Used by permission of Marguerite Stoughton.

You do it through me!" *

Marguerite says that the result of that prayer was not only immediate but incredible. She experienced a tremendous flow of love, peace, and joy that permeated her soul and, two weeks later, when the killers were found, she was able to face them. Only then did she and her family discover that the two murderers had originally planned to force their daughter back into the house where they were going to kill the entire family. Somehow this young woman was able to divert them from their original purpose so that her loved ones were spared.

Even after she learned this, Marguerite allowed God's grace to flow through her, enabling real *forgiveness* to be extended to these diabolical offenders. She and her family continue to pray that these men might someday know the salvation that Jesus has already obtained for them. Furthermore, her five other children have learned from their mother how to recover from grief.

Contrast the beauty of Marguerite's life with that of Melinda. Melinda's nineteen-year-old son, a talented athlete, was killed when a drunk driver lost control of his vehicle and struck the automobile her son was driving. Burdened by overwhelming grief, Melinda has displayed neither solid faith in the Lord nor positive coping mechanisms as an example for her other two children. The end result is that the entire family has disintegrated.

Her older son John feels tremendous guilt because he had been with his brother shortly before the accident and didn't warn him not to go. Of course, he's blaming himself for an incident that was totally out of his control. As he continues to dwell on that night, more and more of his life has been obliterated by remorse and eventually even

*Ibid.

his own marriage ended.

While Melinda busily turns her destructive gaze inward, her health is slowly being destroyed. Presently she is threatening suicide. If she follows through with her plan to self-destruct, perhaps what is left of this grieving little huddle of people will also succumb.

Why can't Melinda see what Marguerite sees? The answer is this: She isn't looking at the person of Christ, the One who longs to enfold her with compassion, listen to her sobbing, and wipe away her tears. He never planned to leave her without assistance, but she can't see that. He showed her, through His own grief, that He cared, but she isn't reading His Word, talking to Him, or conversing with those who know Him intimately.

Instead, she's living in *isolation.* The evil one, Satan, knows that if he can manage to make us feel *alone and abandoned,* then he can continue to hammer away at our minds, making us believe that even God has forsaken us. But is that what the Bible teaches?

Jesus said, "I will not leave you as orphans; I will come to you." (John 14:18) Do you at times feel abandoned in your grief? Orphaned?

Consider Paul, the apostle chosen by Christ, who suffered more than most of us ever will in our lifetime. Despite his many trials, Paul did not become bitter. He was also careful not to fall prey to Satan's lies. Instead, Paul chose to believe: "Blessed *be* the God and Father of our Lord Jesus Christ, the Father of mercies and God of all comfort; who comforts us in all our affliction so that we may be able to comfort those who are in any affliction with the comfort with which we ourselves are comforted by God." (2 Corinthians 1:3, 4)

Paul saw Christ's comfort in every situation and that

knowledge provided him with the courage to continue. It's the same outlook that enables Marguerite to display joy in her life. Christ's strength has kept her from becoming entangled in grief, allowing her instead to walk through it! *None of us can give away what we do not possess. Christ's equipping in our life is a choice.*

Another purpose for grief is that it *builds character* in our lives. As the apostles watched Christ suffer, grief added a believable depth to His personality. If He had come to earth and not allowed Himself to undergo the same painful and wrenching situations that we go through, we could not readily accept that He comprehends our grief. What would make us run to Him for comfort?

We need to know that when someone dies we grieve not only for their physical presence, but also for how they fit into the puzzle of our own life. We were all born to interact with one another and when their piece of our life puzzle is missing, we feel what we believe is an unfillable void. (An entire chapter will be devoted to this subject later in the book.)

When Christ died on the cross, the apostles had to learn to relate to Him in a new way. They could no longer see Him, but they could remember His words, recall His encouragement, and relive in their minds a wealth of miracles. The disciples were able to continue, in spite of their grief, by *dwelling on the gifts* Jesus had left behind. The very words Jesus had spoken to them would sustain them until they met Him again in heaven.

When our own loved ones go on ahead of us to experience their eternal glory with Christ, we need to concentrate not on the fact that they are gone, but rather on what they have left behind of themselves. None of the kindness, love, tenderness, or caring is wasted unless we grieve to the extent that we can no longer see it.

But we don't know how to let go, to that degree. So, instead, we continue to wish to have things back, just the way they were before death altered our hopes, dashed our dreams, and rearranged our lives.

We desire to rewrite the story of our life and make up our own ending. This fight for *control of circumstances* has caused many to quit walking with the Lord. When the God they worship can't be equated as a "celestial Santa Claus," they want to dump Him.

Peter experienced that kind of faith crisis. Do you remember when Christ was teaching the apostles about what *real communion* with Him meant, to partake fully of Him, as the *bread of life*? This saying was difficult for the Jews to understand and many turned away. So Jesus asked Peter and the rest of the twelve if they also wished to leave. "Simon Peter answered Him, 'Lord, to whom shall we go? You have words of eternal life.'" (John 6:68)

In other words, Christ presented a dilemma to Peter and the rest of the disciples. He wanted to know if they were willing to allow Him to *be God* and accept life on His terms, even when He said hard things they could not understand. Peter's profound answer to the question bears repeating! "Lord, to whom shall we go? You have words of eternal life."

What has Christ asked you to accept or give up? A child? A parent? A career? Or a mate? The real question here is one of *trust*. Do you know in the deepest part of your heart that Christ is acting in your behalf? Or are you a person who has difficulty accepting anything that's out of your control? Can you get to the place where, like Marguerite, your response can become one of acceptance?

As we *accept* God's will in our lives, we gain *under-*

standing of Him. Those who say the Serenity Prayer at the end of their Twelve-Step Recovery meetings know what it means to accept what they cannot perceive. And *peace* follows. When we grieve we feel as though we're dangling from a cliff, hollering for help, and no one hears our screams. Yet is that the picture of a loving God who not only created us, but died for our sins? If we can believe Him for something as weighty as where we will spend eternity, then why can't we see that He is ready to act on our pain as well?

Perhaps we don't trust His decisions, especially concerning our present grief, because we don't fully understand His character. We cannot *localize our pain* if we don't know, with every fiber of our being, that *He cares.* One slender book in my library, *Knowledge of the Holy* by A.W. Tozer, has enabled me to grasp the essence of God's attributes.* I've read it so many times that the pages are coming loose from the binding and there are numerous coffee stains throughout. Yet Tozer's mark on my soul through his writing has been indelible.

Tozer has helped me see the *unicity* of God, and therefore to trust Him more deeply. For it is only when we try to reduce God to human terms that we become confused about His ability to operate in our behalf. We can only fully trust someone we comprehend. Understanding that God always acts like Himself—loving, compassionate, faithful, fair, merciful, just, wise, holy, and immutable—provides real comfort for our grieving spirits.

Christ did His best to enable those who heard Him to prepare for His earthly departure. He said, "For a little while longer I am with you, then I go to Him who sent Me." (John 7:33) The Pharisees, chief priests, and the

---

*See Bibliography.

multitudes who listened totally missed the point. God became a man to show us how to live in a world filled with grief. He raised the dead, alleviated the physical pain of those who suffered ailments, loved the unlovable, spent time in a frail human body, and died a despicable death on the cross just so they could be certain of the ultimate degree of His love. Yet they failed to recognize who He was.

Are we doing any better at understanding His life than those first-century witnesses? If we know Christ as the Lord of our lives, then He has to make a difference in how we view our grief. Are you ready to localize your pain to Him? Are you ready to allow Him to exchange the tears from your eyes for a deeper knowledge of His love for you?

4

Cartons of Care

You can't heal a wound by saying it's not there.
Yet the priests and prophets give assurance of peace
when all is war. (Jeremiah 6:14, The Living Bible)

Some wounds demand only a Band-Aid while others need
a tourniquet to stop the bleeding. Likewise, when dealing
with grief we must ascertain not only the *size* of our wound
but also its *origin*. In doing this we can discover the kind
of attention necessary to heal our pain.

This journey will naturally be a process. Perhaps the
most crucial lesson any of us can learn is how to grieve
one thing at a time. Most of us are trying to plow through
the blizzard of our lives with a gigantic snow blower.
Sometimes, though, we need to slow down and use a simple
shovel lest we overlook a gem of understanding that might
be buried under a drift of events and emotions.

How did Christ continue in His ministry when His own
heart was broken? To answer this question we must first
scrutinize not only the familial relationship Jesus had with
his earthly cousin, John the Baptist, but also their dove-
tailed ministries.

John's own birth had been miraculous. We know that
his mother, Elizabeth, was both barren and advanced in

years. While his father, Zacharias, was a priest. On one particular day, while not expecting anything out of the ordinary, Zacharias performed his dutiful service of entering the temple of the Lord and burning incense.

Meanwhile a multitude of people had gathered outside the temple to pray. They, too, were unaware that this specific moment would forever alter a man whose heart was consumed with grief. Indeed, Zacharias had borne the stigma of being without a son and an heir in an extremely family-oriented culture.

Yet where did the angel of the Lord find Zacharias? He certainly hadn't given up on God or turned away simply because his prayers hadn't been answered the way he wanted. Instead, he faithfully executed his prescribed and appointed orders.

Seeing this heavenly being must have scared Zacharias half to death for Gabriel had to admonish him not to be fearful. Then the angel articulated the message that Zacharias's ears had longed to hear: ". . .your petition has been heard, and your wife Elizabeth will bear you a son, and you will give him the name John. And you will have joy and gladness, and many will rejoice at his birth." (Luke 1:13, 14)

John's God-ordained call in life was to be the one who would proclaim Christ as the very "Lamb of God who takes away the sin of the world!" (John 1:29) Had John the Baptist ever wondered about Jesus' true identity? If so, we can rest assured that question was forever settled by God's confirmation of Jesus' authenticity. This occurred at the exact moment in which God's Spirit rested upon Jesus, announcing Him as the Son of God. (John1:30-34)*

---

*See Warren W. Wiersbe, *Bible Exposition Commentary, Be Series,* vol. 1, Matthew - Galatians, Victor Books, 1989, pp. 287-88.

As cousins, John and Jesus had grown up with love for each other. Their mothers were close and we know their families rejoiced at one another's good tidings. For example, no sooner had the angel Gabriel proclaimed Mary would bear the Messiah than she "arose and went with haste to the hill country, to a city of Judah, and entered the house of Zacharias and greeted Elizabeth." (Luke 1:39, 40)

God had uniquely prepared John for his life task. Again in the Gospel of Luke we read the words of the angel Gabriel concerning John's exceptional objective: "For he will be great in the sight of the Lord, and he will drink no wine or liquor; and he will be filled with the Holy Spirit, while yet in his mother's womb. And he will turn back many of the sons of Israel to the Lord their God. And it is he who will go *as a forerunner* before Him in the spirit and power of Elijah, TO TURN THE HEARTS OF THE FATHERS BACK TO THE CHILDREN, and the disobedient to the attitude of the righteous; so as to make ready a people prepared for the Lord." (Luke 1:15-17)

The sand-swept, arid, hostile surroundings of the desert nurtured and fortified John's body, while God used this stark boot camp to strengthen his spirit. We read that John lived there "until the day of his public appearance to Israel." (Luke 1:80)

In the wilderness John had preached repentance and prepared hearts to receive the Messiah. What thoughts must have entertained Zacharias as his son arrived on the Jerusalem scene all decked out in "a garment of camel's hair, and a leather belt about his waist; and his food was locusts and wild honey?" (Matthew 3:4)

In today's vernacular Zacharias probably shook his head and muttered to himself, "What's wrong with this picture?" Things hadn't turned out exactly as he had planned. Yes, God had answered his prayer for a son, but what kind of son was he?

However, this godly family was accustomed to following the voice of God. They willingly sacrificed their own wants and desires, regardless of personal cost. In addition to John's father being a priest in the temple, Elizabeth, his mother, was a descendant of the "daughters of Aaron" (Luke 1:5), from whom the royal line of priests flowed. Jesus' earthly mother, Mary, could trace her own heritage to King David.

Jesus knew that the same austere terrain that had been John's training ground would also be the site of His own preparation for ministry. Immediately after John baptized Him in the Jordan, Jesus Christ was "led up by the Spirit into the wilderness to be tempted by the devil." (Matthew 4:1)

Subsequently John encouraged his own followers to begin looking to Jesus. John the Baptist had fulfilled Isaiah's prophecy and the "voice in the wilderness" (Isaiah 40:3) would now begin to diminish willingly until it would finally be silenced. Although the disciples did their best to soften the blow, the harsh reality of Herod Antipas' vengeful anger and John's imprisonment, as well as the brutal account of John's death, grieved Jesus. At a drunken feast Herodias, the wife of Herod Antipas, had encouraged her daughter Salome to perform a seductive dance, knowing this gesture would exact a price. On instruction from her mother, Salome required as payment the head of John the Baptist on a platter.

How could Jesus endure such cruel treatment of His precious kinsman, a man who had been miraculously born just so that he could herald the arrival of the Messiah?

John had lived the same kind of life his father Zacharias had modeled before him, one of quiet compliance to the will of God.

Jesus' response was to continue in His own ministry, training those who were to carry the message of hope to a needy world when He was no longer physically present. But he never lost sight of the fact that those who chose to live in unbelief were now planning their strategy for killing Him, too. Indeed, the denial of truth had been the underlying cause that allowed the senseless murder of every prophet God had sent in the past.

"For a good work we do not stone You, but for blasphemy; and because You, being a man, make Yourself out *to be* God." (John10:33) Jesus, however, eluded their grasp: "And He went away again beyond the Jordan to the place where John was first baptizing; and He was staying there." (John 10:40)

Why did Jesus return to what was probably the last place He had seen John alive? Perhaps the imminence of His own death made Him remember this special time and the depth of John's personal sacrifice.

During our own grieving process each of us reflects on our last moments with loved ones. We consider their favorite songs, movies, colors, and even that special chair they occupied within our homes. As one friend of mine recently expressed over the loss of her son, "I just want to hug him again." But if God did grant her wish she would soon realize her foolishness. That moment of tenderness would be overshadowed by her desire once again that the young man's cancer-ravaged body would be at peace with Jesus and not gasping for each new breath.

What we really want is to have our loved ones back *whole and healthy*. We can only surmise that Jesus felt

49

this same wrenching emotional tug on His own heart. Jesus had come to the same conclusion all of us do when we accept death for what it is, the due penalty of sin. Herod's exercise of his free will to sin had caused the death of John the Baptist. Yet God reigned sovereignly over the timing of John's death. His task now finished, John would be quickly ushered into the glory God had prepared for him.

Jesus could bear the loss, pain, and grief of John's death because His own foretold death on the cross would make all the difference. John's voice in the wilderness would never be truly stilled. The prophet Isaiah predicted John's birth, name, purpose, and message 600 years before John's birth (Isaiah 40:3) and now God's plan was completed, as He had ordained. It always is!

The record of how Jesus handled John's murder is written and recorded for us to read today. How does this message make a difference in your life? First, Jesus demonstrates that the grieving process *takes time*. After all, three years after John's murder Jesus returned to the place He had last seen John. In addition, *grieving cannot become the central focus of our lives*. We must go on to fulfill our own God-ordained purpose on this earth.

Reverend Jack McGinnis shared his own pain-woven travels at the Steps '92 Conference for the National Association for Christian Recovery (NACR) in Costa Mesa, California.* The amount of real tragedy surrounding his life would be hard to top, even for a weekly soap opera.

At the age of five, his mother abandoned their dysfunctional family. Five years later, his father died in a horren-

---

* For a copy of Rev. McGinnis's lecture, "Recovering from Grief," Steps '92, write The Meadows, P.O. Box 637, Wickenburg, AZ 85358. For more information on this Twelve-Step Christian recovery movement, write NACR, P.O. Box 11095, Whittier CA 90603.

dous fire ignited when his lighted cigarette fell into the sofa. Young Jack and his brother were unable to save their father and barely escaped with their own lives. Consequently, guilt became added to his existing measure of grief.

Now orphaned, Jack was raised by an aunt and uncle who taught him by their example that the way to rid oneself of feelings was to stay busy. This repression of emotions provided a catalyst for his ensuing alcoholism by the age of thirteen.

Substance abuse followed, providing Jack a dangerously false sense of power and belonging, as well as canceling out his heart's obvious anguish. Completely dysfunctional by 1963, Jack then entered the priesthood where he also became incapable of responding to the emotional needs of his parishioners. For many within the audience who had grown up with the idea that members of the clergy "had their act together," Jack's testimony shows in stark terms we cannot place labels of perfection on any human being. For all of us, life contains challenges, pits, traps, and snares that can propel us into the loving and rescuing arms of Jesus as we search for a way out of our grief.

At the core of Reverend McGinnis's dank well of grief was the physical and emotional loss of his mother. He related how he would pick up the phone and ask the operator to "find his mother" so that he could speak with her. In this town where the operator knew everyone, she indeed was able to locate his mother. Momentarily soothed by the sound of her voice, Jack would soon be assaulted by a deep sense of abandonment once he cradled the deathly silent receiver again.

Let's repeat Jeremiah 6:14: "You cannot heal a wound by saying it's not there." These words were written while

Jerusalem was under siege. God had warned the Israelites repeatedly that they would bring punishment down on their own heads if they refused to worship Him and turned instead to idols. Incredibly, the Israelites opted to listen to the lying utterances of their religious leaders who sugarcoated their sin, ignored what was wrong, and required no change from them.

Has a portion of your grief included a self-inflicted wound? Have you pretended that bonding between loved ones never occurred as you walked out of their lives to seek your own happiness? Is there someone in your past who is languishing, all the while anticipating the reassuring sound of your voice? Are you now willing to set prior pain and hurt aside long enough to know that a call or an apology might release them to begin their own recovery from grief?

If we continue to turn a deaf ear to the pain and grief that we have bundled up and delivered as an excruciating burden for others to bear, we will never be free of the weight of our own grief. No matter how much hurt we have endured, we cannot condone the harm we have leveled at another.

From Reverend McGinnis's childhood grief we see the importance of understanding and empathy. These deep, gaping wounds from childhood do remain with us. Lurking like shadowed, grotesque figures, they intrude on the rest of our lives.

On the heels of the loss of his parents, Jack McGinnis was ushered not only into another dysfunctional home but also a place that restrained his expression of grief. Perhaps this was an acceptable outlook during the 1940s and 50s but we are now many years beyond that. Adults are finally beginning to remove the lids on their containers of repressed grief. But are we recognizing that children partake of life's agonies with the same depth as adults? Do we expect them to endure silently the atrocities visited upon them as good little soldiers in an unfair war?*

Emma, a small and sickly girl, understood grief at an early age when she contracted rheumatic fever as the result of a lingering case of strep throat. Back in the late 1940s the prescription for her recovery was a year of bed rest. At the age of four this seemed more like a prison sentence, with her upstairs bedroom window becoming her only access to the outside world.

Along with the consuming sense of isolation came Emma's first acquaintance with an emotion called loneliness. Since she could not participate in her large family's routine activities, she became introspective, investigative, and inventive. Unable to read, she mastered steadiness of hand for coloring and artwork, learned creative ways to fill large blocks of time, and accepted her own company as being sufficient. These skills became the nucleus for her career as a painter, her creative expression as a poet, and also her training to be a writer.

Had her time been spent resenting these early circumstances of life, she would never have acquired the proficiency her life choices demanded. But before we bestow too much credit on Emma, let's remember that it was the Lord who not only sanctioned the timing for her debilitating illness but provided the way through it.

Although our first and most normal response is to flee from the source of our agony, we must constrain ourselves to follow the example of Jesus Christ, continue in our pur-

---

* Christine Harder Tangvald is a prolific author, seminar speaker, and teacher who manages to reach into the hearts of children, creating a release for their pent-up fears and worries. Through her books (see Bibliography), children can get in touch with grief-producing episodes in their lives.

pose, and walk down the path He has chosen for us despite our grief-producing episodes. The alternative is to waste this precious gift of life we possess.

According to a newspaper article, a young woman in her mid-thirties died the *second* time she plunged from a bridge in the Northwest.* However, her friends relate that it was the first time she plunged from the bridge, nearly two decades earlier, that really killed her.

To recount the initial events, she was barely eighteen and her sister even younger when they stopped at a local market one autumn day. While in the store two men fiendishly disabled their car and as the girls emerged from the store the evil pair offered to take them home. Instead, the men drove the girls to a remote bridge that spanned high above a rapidly flowing river. There the older girl was brutally raped and beaten, and later both girls were tossed over the bridge, causing them to fall into the narrow gorge below.

The younger one dropped straight down, hit her head on a rock at the edge of the river bank, and died instantly. But the older one's fall had been broken when she slammed against the bridge's structure and into a ledge. This not only placed her body into deeper water but also fractured her leg. Amazingly, she managed to swim to the shore and the following morning, after she was sure her abductors had fled, crawled to the roadside where she was found and rescued. That same day her abductors were arrested, and later they were tried and convicted and given death sentences that were subsequently commuted to life in prison.

Though given another chance at life herself, the surviv-

*"Second Fall Makes Woman's Death Complete," *The Orange County Register,* August 23, 1992, page A8.

ing sister seemed powerless to surmount her overwhelming grief over her sister's death. She also became increasingly incapable of accepting the fact of her own survival. Those closest to her told how during what turned out to be the last week of her life she had repeatedly viewed a movie about a dismal suicide. This story of a man who couldn't cope with memories of being molested and who eventually succumbed to death had an obvious effect on her.

The young woman returned to what had become for her life's most unforgettable moment. At first she walked with her boyfriend and small daughter alongside the waist-high railing of the bridge. Then she sat with her legs dangling through that same railing while resting her arms on top as she recounted aloud the tragic events that had transpired there years before. Tearfully she verbalized the love she felt for her boyfriend. He responded by saying something about not wanting the little girl to watch her cry. As he turned to walk her small child back to the car, he suddenly heard a sound and turned. Her body had crashed into the water and the deafening, eerie sound echoed against the nearby canyon walls.

Looking at this lovely woman's newspaper photo, one is quickly drawn to her bright, cheery smile. Yet she could not surmount her grief and trade those tormented memories for the gift of peace. How easily our hearts fill with compassion for a family that has lost two of their precious children at this same bridge.

Her story could belong to any of us. Horror, violence, sin, and senseless murder were as much a part of Christ's society as they are of ours. Yet He found a way to withstand this grief. And He is certainly capable of developing coping mechanisms within us, too. The question is, will we allow Him the freedom to work in our lives?

5

Abandoned Attachés

My God, My God, why has Thou forsaken Me?
(Matthew 27:46)

Did a feeling of pure despair prompt Christ to cry out these words from the cross? No, not really, for He never stopped being God the Son. Jesus experienced separation from God when He voiced these words, but He had *willingly* shouldered this burden of momentary estrangement. There was no other way to pay for all of our sins than to take them upon Himself.

Jesus Christ became the Father's Lamb, the perfect sacrifice, in our behalf. During those six hours in which His body hung upon the cross, He did endure the emotion of "being forsaken" by the Father. Sin makes us feel the same way, but it's never God who walks away. When we choose to act contrary to His commandments and willfully sin, we are the ones who break the fellowship God freely offers. That horrible, shameful, black hole called *separation from God*—experienced by Jesus on the cross—occurs because our *holy, all-good, perfect God* cannot look upon sin.

However, the words Jesus spoke from the cross also fulfilled Scripture: They are the beginning of Psalm 22, a prophetic passage concerning the Messiah's death. Every word Jesus uttered from the cross takes on new meaning when we understand this. We cannot minimize the weight of agony as He chose to leave the Garden of Gethsemane and go to the cross for us. But it's also imperative that we see the underlying purpose for His ultimate sacrifice.

Jesus allowed Himself to become fully involved with grief and estrangement, the result of sin, so that He could empathize with the human condition. He sees when you've crossed over every line in the sand you've ever drawn, and when you've slipped so far into sin that you're not sure there's any plausible way back to sanity. That's the point at which we assume He's gone and doesn't ever want to hear from us again. This directly correlates with the moment in which we *quit praying* and withdraw even further into the dregs of inhumanity.

Where is He during this tumultuous array of emotions? Right there beside you, with His arms outstretched, saying, "Come to Me, all who are weary and heavy-laden, and I will give you rest. Take My yoke upon you, and learn from Me, for I am gentle and humble in heart; and YOU SHALL FIND REST FOR YOUR SOULS." (Matthew 11:28-30)

Isolation and grief are a deadly mixture, evidenced by the stories shared in the previous chapter. If the distressed person doesn't obtain help from those around them, it's possible that they may plummet into a spiral of depression from which they will find no recovery. Many times the burden and agony of grief become like a suitcase that is too weighty to carry anymore. At this point, the afflicted person may opt not only to lighten life's satchel of trials but forsake the burdensome trunk altogether. In other words, he or she may contemplate suicide. In turn each person close to them will be tempted to assume an unwarranted load of guilt, thereby placing themselves in jeopardy, too.

Where does the cycle stop? Obviously, at the point of initial pain. By understanding the warning signs of suicide, we can assist our friends and loved ones in developing coping mechanisms.

A rifle shot reverberated through a quiet, residential beach community in southern California. Only then did the neighbors realize the depth of despair to which one man in his sixties had plunged. Police summoned his wife from the hospital where she worked and quickly assigned her the gruesome task of identifying his body. While viewing his disfiguring, warlike injuries, reality staggered in like a voracious monster.

She had lovingly cared for her husband throughout his many months of sickness. Both patient and caregiver had seemingly accepted the fact that the end was not far off. So why did he hasten his time? Were there warning signs she missed?

He had *talked about suicide*, one of the warning signs, but she hadn't considered the conversations seriously. Now she will forever feel cheated out of the time she had hoped to spend with her husband. To alleviate his suffering she had offered him solace, companionship, and skilled nursing. But she never had the chance to say goodbye.

Why wasn't this man able to accept the comfort his spouse lovingly offered and ease into the transition from life to death? We can only guess that he bought into Satan's systemized lie that suicide would somehow alleviate his anguish. Upon crossing over his pain threshold, he began believing that *he* and not God knew when he'd had enough.

Perhaps this seduction of thoughts appeared subtle at

first, with a message such as, "Maybe I should just end it all." Although at first he probably dismissed these thoughts, after several months of bombardment, he grew accustomed to the idea, conditioned to the facts, and accepting of the concept. For once we *acquiesce to Satan's lie* we're halfway to carrying it out; the devil's powers of persuasion are so great his thoughts seem like our own. At that point the suicidal person transfers into the *planning stage* of their demise.

They become more *secretive verbally*, another warning sign, and one must begin to *interpret their actions* instead. They may *begin giving away possessions* and *withdrawing from things that formerly gave them pleasure.* They appear *bored or disinterested. Changes in eating or sleeping habits, a decline in productivity level at work or school, violent behavior, and obvious personality changes may also be observed.* * Watch these signs carefully and then get help. Don't wait for all the signs to be present before taking action. It may be too late!

Satan's strategy then shifts to one of attempting to *keep anyone with the truth away from the suicide candidate.* Have you ever had a scary or unsettling feeling about someone and not taken action on it, only later to discover this person had met a terrible fate? God was alerting you to pray with intensity and persistence.

Many years ago I experienced a dream in which a friend was seated at the desk in his office, the agony of defeat and desperation distorting his face. With eyes glazed over he slowly pulled open the top drawer of his walnut desk and wrapped his hand around the cold steel of a small handgun. I screamed to stop him, awakening suddenly

---

*Greg Laurie, "The Ultimate Wipeout—The Epidemic of Teenage Suicide," *Harvest* magazine, Summer 1985, pp. 8-11.

from the dream. After inquiring what was wrong, my husband minimized the importance of my unwelcome movie reel and admonished me to "just go back to sleep."

However, the urgency to pray had already kicked in and I did indeed spend most of the rest of the night in supplication to the Lord to surround our friend with angels and protect him from harm. In the morning I prayed about whether to write or telephone, not knowing how imminent this crisis might be. The assurance that a letter would be appropriate brought me peace. I had to rely on the Lord for the right words. How do you relate to a good friend that you know they're depressed enough to commit suicide when you haven't seen them in months?

Immediately I wrote that no matter what situation existed, it certainly couldn't be hopeless because God had reached out to those who loved this person, soliciting prayers in his behalf. Within a couple of days I received a written response from this man's wife that included this sentence: "Only the Holy Spirit could have told you that we were going through the dark night of the soul!"

Although I've never been privy to the exact nature of his trial, I'm aware that God allowed that dream to produce the urgency necessary to keep me awake and praying. Knowing He cares that deeply about our loneliness and pain is confirmation enough that our God is conscious of our every need.

Somehow we can come to grips with the untimely demise of a loved one. However, since 1955 the number of young people opting to end their lives rather than seek workable solutions has tripled.* Why would so many in the prime of their lives wish to end it all? Without attempting to oversimplify the answer, they believe Satan's

*Ibid.

progressive lie that there is, in reality, no hope!

You are born *with a God-given purpose* that Satan will attempt to thwart until your dying day. He desires to hinder you from finding Christ and learning what real life is. At the same time, he will ultimately settle for your hasty death, especially by your own hand. Such a tragedy is preferred by Satan because untold grief, confusion, unanswered questions, and, most important, doubt about God are heaped on those left behind.

We need only to follow the Gospel accounts of Jesus' ministry to know that the same tactics Satan chooses to wreak havoc on us were also applied to Christ. The most well-known encounter is Satan's temptation of Christ in the wilderness (Matthew 4:1-11), but he also played a role in inciting people against Him and, ultimately, hoped to keep Christ from the cross, by which we all have the hope of obtaining *salvation.*

A tragic accident lessened Satan's hold on my life. While speeding down an icy mountain slope, the saucer sled on which I had become airborne crashed back to earth with such force that I suffered a compression fracture below my shoulder blades. Over the next nine months of recovery I had nowhere to look but up and I finally committed my life to Christ.

Working for me during that time was a short one-liner I had memorized as a child from the *Baltimore Catechism*. The question, "Why were you born?" was followed by this answer: "To know, love, and serve God."

Although years had passed since I had pondered these poignant words, the sudden realization that I really didn't *know Him* initiated within me an earnest search. That probe ended one day at a Bible study I never planned on attending. My neighbor, Cheryl Dunnam, had lovingly

showered me with her time and attention during my recu-
peration. I just couldn't say no to her warm invitation
again.

When the study leader read the words of First
Corinthians 12:3, my body felt as if it had just been zapped
by lightning. Later, this teacher related why this verse of
Scripture had such a profound effect on me.

No one could have realized my present depth of depression—I was too skillful at repressing it—and that deep
within my private hell was a conglomeration of things for
which I blamed and rebuked God. The most recent, of
course, was my severe back injury. I reasoned that if He
were God, why didn't He stop the accident from happening in the first place? Only later would I come to understand that this particular incident was the springboard to
new life for me, in Christ.

There also existed a deep *sense of grief* that I could not
attach to anything in particular. Considering simply the
exterior trimmings of my life, there was much for others
to envy. I had married the man I truly loved and the marriage had lasted. While he was on active duty in the army
we had traveled to many exciting places, and now, settled
in a home, we had three beautiful children. Yet all the
while a *gnawing, empty feeling pervaded my life,* creating an intolerable sense of grief. Each time this conviction reared its abominable head, I would rationalize it away,
never coming to grips with its source.

Finally, while hearing the Scripture read that day at the
study, I learned for the first time that I would never be
able to know God without the *power of the Holy Spirit
dwelling inside of me*. Although it took almost three
months for me to make a public commitment, during that
time I continued to interview and investigate the testimo-

nies of others who had found a real and workable relationship with God. On Father's Day, 1973, I finally answered the pastor's invitation from the pulpit to commit my life to Christ.

The first noticeable change in my life was this incredible perception of *not being alone*, as though a treasured friend accompanied me everywhere. Perhaps what I needed from God at that time was a sense of *belonging to Him*, but after all these years His presence is still the most precious asset in my life. Just as it took me a long time to understand who Jesus was, there were those during His time on earth whose spiritual blindness prevented them from accepting His inevitable death. Although Jesus had repeatedly said that *He came from the Father* and would *return to the Father*, the religious leaders didn't get it. "Where does this man intend to go that we shall not find Him?" (John 7:35) "Surely He will not kill Himself, will He, since He says, 'Where I am going, you cannot come'?" (John 8:22)

How could Jesus possibly disappear from the face of the earth? And by what *human means* could He continue to elude their grasp? Therein lies the answer. Jesus planned to lay down His life *willingly* so that we could all someday partake of paradise with Him.

However, this extraterrestrial experience hinges on a twofold truth: "And without faith it is impossible to please *Him*, for he who comes to God must believe that He is, and *that* He is the rewarder of those who seek Him." (Hebrews 11:6) Did your loved ones die with this knowledge and belief? If the answer is a definitive yes, then you can rest with the assurance that they are with Jesus.

The reverse is a terrible truth: If the answer to this most important life question is no, then they are not with Him.

There are no other options. Acts 4:12 clearly states, "And there is salvation in no one else; for there is no other name under heaven that has been given among men, by which we must be saved." Jesus already accomplished all the hard work of salvation.

How can you cope with the awareness that someone you loved and cared about died and didn't know Christ? The cross of that knowledge is likely the heaviest anyone on earth will bear because it is weighted by grief and helplessness. (See Luke 16:22-26.) Speaking of suicide always seems to evoke this question. Suicide is, in effect, "self murder," but murder, a horrendous sin and rebuke of God's great gift of life, is not the one sin that Christ said would keep us out of heaven.

In Luke 12:10 Jesus says, "And everyone who will speak a word against the Son of Man, it shall be forgiven him; but he who blasphemes against the Holy Spirit, it shall not be forgiven him." Blasphemy against the Holy Spirit is *refusing to attribute salvation as the work of God's Spirit*, accomplished by Christ on the cross. It is to either say or internalize that Christ's death is meaningless and cannot affect our eternal destiny.

Are there Christians who commit suicide? Probably. Just because we are sure of our eternal destiny doesn't mean that we are free of Satan's lies, pressures, and temptations. If we can still be tempted to sin in every other area after making our commitment to Christ, why do we think that suicide is off limits?

On the other hand, to say that hell is the automatic destination of all suicide victims would intimate that we as humans have knowledge that belongs solely to God. Consider many existing medications, some as subtle as mild tranquilizers, that can cause severe depression, thereby robbing a person of rational thinking. In the moments before an overdose, Satan's heinous lies about "ending it all" have never seemed as seductive. Only Satan could assure these troubled individuals they are desperately and utterly alone and unloved.

The Christian who succumbs to the sin of suicide has forever lost his or her opportunity to affect lives on earth with the Gospel. They have refused to trust our loving God for the plan He had ready to implement in their lives; they have refused to exchange their desperation for His aspirations. But the God we worship is not heartless. He alone knows whether something has interfered with a person's ability to make a free and cognitive choice or if they have unwittingly succumbed to something beyond their control.

In Psalm 103:13, 14 we read, "Just as a father has compassion on *his* children, so the LORD has compassion on those who fear Him. For He Himself knows our frame; He is mindful that we are *but* dust." We also have a clarifying promise in Romans 8:38, 39: "For I am convinced that neither death, nor life, nor angels, nor principalities, nor things present, nor things to come, nor powers, nor height, nor depth, nor any other created thing, shall be able to separate us from the love of God, which is in Christ Jesus our Lord." This century's great evangelist, Billy Graham, has used these same Scriptures in his book, *Answers To Life's Problems* (see Bibliography), when discussing suicide.

We must begin to realize that at the same time our fragile and confused minds are being barraged by Satan's sinister attacks, God Himself is trying to break through with His message of concern and confirmation. How can we listen to that *still small voice*, the voice that has commanded patriarchs, prophets, and pastors?

First, by staying in touch with God through *daily prayer and Scripture reading*. If we are in the Word, the storms of life may toss us precariously about but we won't be thrown overboard without a life preserver. Jesus will be right there, using the power of His Word—the power of the Resurrection—to enable us to live through our trials.

Second, we need to *surround ourselves with Christians* who can assist us in a crisis. If a drowning man refuses to reach out for a life preserver, he will surely die. Our godly friends continue to be our lifeline as long as we're honest with them about our fears and foibles, allowing them to intervene in our lives when we have lost our perspective.

Third, we must learn to *accept the help of others*. This is no easy task. In a preelection interview with David Frost, former Senator Albert Gore was asked how his family coped during his son's recovery from a serious accident.* Senator Gore responded that the people who helped their family the most were those who had also suffered the most. This had come as quite a surprise to him, as it would to most of us, since we feel that only strength can benefit us during times of greatest weakness and vulnerability.

Yet whom did God choose to bolster the Gore family? Those who had received Christ's ministrations were chosen. That's the purpose of our suffering: to reach out and strengthen those in pain, to bring news of Jesus' light and life to those who are lonely or despairing, and to comfort others as Christ Himself has consoled us.

Jesus Christ has provided specific ways to distinguish His voice from those who might condemn or confuse us. Satan attempts to *convince* us we're isolated, unloved, and without hope; God *clarifies* our path and, at times, may

*Aired October 6, 1992.

convict us of our sin. However, when the Lord does point out our errors, He always indicates a process by which we can turn things around. And with this *correction* will be a reaffirming of God's standards for our lives. Further, while Satan distorts, minimizes, and obliterates God's laws, the voice of God's Spirit within us naturally draws our thinking back to the One who loves us unconditionally.

Remember Jesus Christ Himself has *chosen* you and His path for you will always coincide with what Scripture teaches. In other words, the direction you receive from Him will never contradict the written Word. Satan, on the other hand, attempts to *capture* those who would believe his lies and follow the path of deception.

While Christ *constrains* us (2 Corinthians 4:6), Satan *constricts* us. But the *true light* will always attempt to shine in whatever darkness we find ourselves, assuring us that we are not alone because He is with us.

Some might ask, "But how does God literally speak to us?" Writer Marilyn Heavilin had an answer during a Christian women's retreat in southern California.* She says that God speaks to us in the areas of affection, reflection, correction, direction, and inspection. "When you hear these thoughts come into your mind," Heavilin said, "write down the message and make sure it does in fact agree with Scripture."

Peter Wagner, in his book *Prayer Shield* (see Bibliography), further admonishes us to spend whatever time is needed in prayer so that we will be sure of God's will in any matter. I've learned over two decades of walking with the Lord that my prayer life cannot be a one-way conver-

---

*Marilyn Heavilin, 1993 Southern California Christian Women's Retreat, prayer seminar notes.

sation in which I just present my "grocery list" to God and expect Him to fill it. Keeping a journal helps me not only to know what I've already shared with my Father, but also provides a written record of the things He's shared with me. These thoughts only flow when I'm silent before Him for a while.

Charles Spurgeon once stated that when we pray we should feel as if we "walk facing Jesus," while C. S. Lewis wrote that prayer is "as though we're dancing in step with Jesus."

No matter how you term this intimate time with your Creator, you will not feel alone, abandoned, or misaligned. Jesus was not forsaken on the cross at all. His sacrifice was God's provision that all men and women throughout history might know that they are loved, forgiven, and treasured. Jesus' Resurrection from the dead is proof that God accepted His offering.

Have you crossed over the bridge between hopelessness and forgiveness by accepting the relationship Christ made possible? Do you fully understand that in His weakest human moment on the cross at Calvary Jesus displayed His greatest strength? Jesus shed His own precious blood so that you could one day join Him in heaven.

6

Footlockers of Loss

For God so loved the world, that He gave His only
begotten Son, that whoever believes in Him should not
perish, but have eternal life. (John 3:16)

Has anyone lost more than God? Initially He created a
perfect world, a lush, vibrant garden paradise called Eden,
where He desired to commune with men and women. The
only figurative sign He "posted" for the two humans who
dwelled within this idyllic habitat read *"Obedience Re-*
quired." Not a bad exchange for a stress-free living ar-
rangement!

Enter that seductive old serpent—Satan in disguise—
and human frailty didn't stand a chance. Adam and Eve,
of course, opted to test God's authority and were promptly
tossed out into the tempestuous world of toil, trials, and
thorns.

We've been in a state of rebellion ever since. (Genesis
3:1-7) If you placed any one of us in Adam and Eve's
position, we wouldn't have fared any better because we
don't desire to adhere to God's requirements 100 percent
of the time. Fortunately, God's nature is not only forgiving but absolutely and totally loving. He sent His Son,
Jesus, to prove to us the depth of His devotion. As the

Good Shepherd, Jesus continues to seek those who choose to become estranged from Him.

This time the loss God suffered proved even more immense. How could He watch as those humans, into whom He had breathed life, demanded the very lifeblood of His only begotten Son? Jesus willingly left His throne, where He had been securely seated beside the Father, to come to earth and withstand untold suffering at the hands of the very people He had created. Can we even comprehend that it was God Himself, in the form of a man, who hung on Calvary's splintered cross?

For the time being, let's back up a bit in history. Throughout His lifespan on earth Christ endured a myriad of other hate-filled demonstrations prior to this final indignation.

He was pursued by the evil Herod who convinced himself that this babe would usurp his throne. Consequently, Herod dispatched troops to murder every male child born during the first two years of Jesus' life. (Matthew 2:16) If only this corrupt king had taken the time to read the record, written by the prophets and inspired by God's very Spirit, he could have shared a reserved place in God's eternal kingdom. Sadly, he resembles men and women of our own time who, driven by ambition, power, and greed, have no time left for seeking the *truth*.

However, the babe of Bethlehem survived. God sent an angel who warned Joseph to flee with his charges, Mary and Jesus, to Egypt and remain there until it was safe to return. (Matthew 2:13) In obedience, Joseph responded and the Father was pleased. After Herod's death an angel again appeared to Joseph. This time the messenger instructed him to return to the land of Israel. In all these events the Word of God, as recorded by the Old Testament prophets, was fulfilled.

For thirty years Jesus remained in relative seclusion as He awaited the Father's perfect timing for His public ministry. In doing so, He demonstrated both submission and cooperation with the will of the Father.

One would imagine that the greatest gift ever delivered would not only be recognized and sought after by all men and women, but also fully accepted by the world. Instead, *because of the message of peace and love He brought,* Christ was maligned, doubted, questioned, rebuked, ignored, and finally the object of retaliation.

What has your own response been to His coming to earth? What kind of reception can He expect as He continues to pursue a cherished place in your heart?

"But there are some of you who do not believe." Jesus knew from the beginning who did not believe, and who it was that would betray Him. Thus He stated, "For this reason I have said to you, that no one can come to Me, unless it has been granted him from the Father." As a result, many of His disciples withdrew and would not walk with Him anymore. (John 6:64-66)

Many could follow Jesus as long as His message didn't become too controversial or require complete dedication. One of His most upsetting statements—in the first century and today—was when He said He had come down from heaven. We can call Jesus a good teacher, or a good man, or a prophet, and the world accepts those labels. But when we admit what He has already stated concerning His origin, the crowd begins to disperse rather quickly. Their own brand of comfortable religion beckons. Rather than reach for an eternal relationship, they plummet back down into the same hopeless state they occupied before hearing the way out!

Perhaps in your youth there existed a time when belief flowed easily. It was before the river of life filled its banks with things to disappoint, disparage, and dispel the dreams you attempted to grasp along the barren shoreline.

Rest assured no one has weathered more grief than our Lord, Jesus Christ, who despite persecution and death on the cross has continued to offer the gift of hope, forgiveness, and eternal life. There is but one plan, one Savior, and one way back to God!

How do we know this? Because of *the promise* Jesus made to God and then shared as a prayer with His beloved disciples in His final moments with them. "Father, I desire that they also whom Thou hast given Me be with Me where I am, in order that they may behold My glory, which Thou hast given Me; for Thou didst love Me before the foundation of the world. O Righteous Father, although the world has not known Thee, yet I have known Thee; and these have known that Thou didst send Me; and I have made Thy name known to them, and will make it known; that the love wherewith Thou didst love Me may be in them, and I in them." (John 17:24-26)

If the luggage you've strained to tote through life has held a duffel bag of disappointments or afflictions, have you drawn a wrongful conclusion about God's love for you? Then consider Stephen, who had every reason to question God's dealings in his life and yet chose to walk in step with his Master. Only those who have skillfully managed the delicate art of *abiding*, of keeping their eyes focused on heaven and yet planting their feet on terra firma, have comprehended the mystery of God's love.

Acts 6 begins with a comparison of the events preceding Christ's own death as Stephen is dragged before the Jewish council. There he is accused by false witnesses who say he spoke against the temple and the law. In reality, Stephen had merely stated the full impact of the risen Christ on both their customs and the laws of Moses, which many of them still clung to. (Acts 6:12-15)

Being confronted by the decision-making members of the council would have struck fear in the heart of any Jew. And yet these men were amazed not only by Stephen's grace and power but also by the signs and wonders he performed. In spite of this intimidating atmosphere, Stephen displayed no fear. Instead, the council observed that his face resembled that of an angel. Didn't Stephen understand their despicable plan?

Keep in mind Stephen had *lived his life for the Gospel* and now he was fully prepared to *give his life* for it. His logical presentation of that Gospel before the council had indeed sealed his fate. Along with his powerful applications of Christ's teachings to the lives of his listeners, which stung their beings to the core, he also exposed their evil motives. For although these religious leaders had received the laws of Moses, they had never obeyed them. If they had, they would have accepted Jesus as their promised Messiah.

The eloquence of Stephen's words cannot be denied: "'You men who are stiffnecked and uncircumcised in heart and ears are always resisting the Holy Spirit; you are doing just as your fathers did. Which one of the prophets did your fathers not persecute? And they killed those who had previously announced the coming of the Righteous One, whose betrayers and murderers you have now become; you who received the law as ordained by angels, and *yet* did not keep it.' Now when they heard this, they were cut to the quick, and they *began* gnashing their teeth at him....But they cried out with a loud voice, and covered their ears, and they rushed upon him with one impulse." (Acts 7:51-54, 57)

With his death at hand, Stephen's actions paralleled Jesus' own on the cross. First, as the men were *stoning him*, Stephen "called upon *the Lord* and said, 'Lord Jesus receive my spirit!'" Falling on his knees, Stephen cried out, "'Lord, do not hold this sin against them!'" (Acts 7:59-60)

What was Stephen's enabling power during this moment of greatest grief? "But being full of the Holy Spirit, he gazed intently into heaven and saw the glory of God, and Jesus standing at the right hand of God; and he said, 'Behold I see the heavens opened up and the Son of Man standing at the right hand of God.'" (Acts 7:55, 56)

Only when we open the eyes of our hearts to *see Jesus,* are we able to endure our greatest trials. Can you hear Christ asking you the same question He put to the disciples: "You do not want to go away also, do you?" (John 6:67) Peter answered Jesus, "Lord, to whom shall we go? You have words of eternal life. And we have believed and have come to know that You are the Holy One of God." (John 6:68, 69) Peter had walked with the Lord long enough to comprehend that there was no one like Him, that He cared, and that He truly had answers to life's tough problems. Stephen understood the same thing. Are you convinced?

Perhaps you have reacted to this beautiful account this way: "Stephen was a pillar of the church, an early saint. People like him were *prepared* to die for Christ. I'm only *trying to live* in this world and be a decent person, and that's hard enough considering the burden of grief I carry."

Consider the life of Corrie ten Boom, dubbed by Billy and Ruth Graham as "God's merry saint." Could life have been more arduous for this author of *The Hiding Place*? In a secret room in their home in Haarlem, Holland, Corrie and her family hid Jewish people from the Nazis during World War II. Subsequently discovered and arrested during the very month and year in which I was born, February of 1944, the ten Booms were banished to a concentration camp. There Corrie's sister, father, brother, and nephew died.

Initially, part of Corrie's own overwhelming grief came from what is termed *survivor's guilt*. Why should her life have been spared when those she loved and considered more godly than herself had been taken? Corrie came to accept the extraordinary fact that God is God and we must learn to fit into His plan and not He into ours. God had an agenda for her life and would enable Corrie to accomplish it, despite every obstacle.

Incredibly, it is because of this dear gray-haired woman of God, who learned to depend on, cleave to, and walk in step with Jesus, that I am a Christian today. During the lengthy recovery from my broken back, I happened to watch a television interview with Corrie ten Boom. In her thick Dutch accent she spoke graphically of the miracles God performed while she was incarcerated in Ravensbruck and she also shared the pain of her sister Betsie's suffering and death. How could she have survived all these atrocities with love, I wondered?

But it was her account of *releasing the temptation to hate* the man who had been responsible for the capture of Corrie's family that pulled at my heartstrings. God used the words of Matthew 6:14, 15 to enable Corrie to forgive this man. Furthermore, when he was sentenced to death following the war, Corrie not only corresponded with this one-time murderer but *she shared the way of salvation!*

Hearing her account left me with two distinct impressions. First, I had not allowed God the freedom to exercise any power over my life through His Word. Second, I was incapable of forgiving to that extent. Corrie ten Boom's story, in effect, became the launching pad of my desire to know Jesus Christ, to be empowered by Him to forgive, and to understand my purpose on earth.

For many people the very depth of grief upon losing a loved one propels them toward Christ. Having flown a great distance to stand vigil beside the deathbed of her precious grandmother, Marie couldn't imagine never seeing her again. Yet the power of Christ within her provided sustenance.

However, this valise of inconsolable grief became too heavy for Marie's eighty-three-year-old grandfather, Alfred, who had been in church and praying all his life and yet had never allowed entrance to Christ's light and life. He knew about God but he didn't have a personal relationship with Jesus.

A true family patriarch, Alfred appeared as unwavering as a mighty oak in a windstorm throughout the planning and implementing of the funeral. After the services, however, Alfred behaved far differently as he proceeded to hurl his grief angrily at family members who had displeased him at one time or another.

Central to his anger was the fact that one of his granddaughters, Marie, had chosen to leave the church she had grown up in and seek a more evangelical congregation. To Alfred, whose entire personal identity had become entwined in this particular church affiliation, the switch was intolerable.

Nothing Marie said or did could dissuade Alfred from this zealous and unyielding position. For him there was only *one church*, the one he chose to belong to. Many times a grieving person will tend to pick the moment when family members' hearts are fragmented to apply the leverage of behavior control. This grieving individual is endeavoring to dominate another's life because their own is turning on its axis and spinning out into a vast and turbulent sphere.

Shortly after this exchange Marie returned home to her own family. Feeling completely severed from both her grandparents' love, she continually prayed to know how to handle this perplexing situation. She tried to concentrate on what life must be like for her grandfather, now totally alone after sixty-two years of marriage. She herself deeply missed the weekly communication from her grandmother, a part of her life for so many years.

After praying, the Lord prompted Marie to send two notes a week to her grandfather, repeating the same words over and over: "I love you and Jesus loves you." But even reaching the six- month "grief milestone" produced nothing but deafening silence from him.

At this point Marie's frustration level skyrocketed. How should she proceed? All attempts to dispel her emotions weren't working and tears of grief flowed freely, spilling out onto her family. "I'll write a letter, Mommy, and tell your grandpa to stop hurting you just because you love Jesus," offered her young daughter. That's when Marie placed her despair at the feet of Christ. "No, we'll wait for His answer, no matter how long it takes," Marie responded to her child.

Unexpectedly, a few days after this encounter with her daughter a pale blue envelope appeared in her mailbox. The return address belonged to Marie's grandfather. His initial note said, "Well, I guess I know that *you love me* and that *Jesus loves me*." Their bonding in Christ has initiated a letter-writing exchange that has bolstered this lonely man through twelve years of grief and also kept their relationship in tact. How much they both would have missed if Marie had allowed her grief to turn to bitterness instead of *trusting God*.

These individuals who have sought refuge in Christ and continued on with life, despite the tragic loss of loved ones, became standards of faith for those around them. Contrasted with Stephen, Corrie ten Boom, and Marie, others choose to wade in the midst of their grief, never to learn the incredible gifts God has for them on the other side of pain.

Is there someone from whom you've become estranged? Perhaps they've slammed the door in your face, as Marie's grandfather, and the possibilities for love seem impossible. Are you willing to pray for a miracle of healing, not only for the sorrow you're feeling at this loss but also for their incredible weight of grief?

Although many have chosen not to respond to God's loving and sacrificial offer of salvation, this in no way diminishes the magnitude of God. His character remains in tact and His unwavering attributes will endure for all of time and eternity. God's arms are still outstretched, just as they were that Good Friday on Calvary, to welcome and receive those who would repent of sin and return to the relationship He desired for them all along.

7

Tossing Your Trunk
of Grief

*And they took offense at Him. But Jesus said to them,
"A prophet is not without honor except in his home
town, and in his own household." (Matthew 13:57)*

Had this Scripture verse served as the basis for a newspaper headline, it probably would have read, "Itinerant Preacher Returns Home to Astonished Crowd." Sometime after John the Baptist's death, Jesus began teaching in the synagogue at Nazareth. (Luke 4:16) Those who had known Him only as the carpenter's son couldn't imagine how He had obtained such wisdom and miraculous powers. After all, they knew His earthly mother, Mary, and His brothers, James, Joseph, Simon, and Judas, and His sisters. (Matthew 13:54-56)

Now He had not only returned, but He was teaching in their local place of worship! Everywhere He went a multitude gathered, begging for healing, signs, and miracles. How did His earthly family respond to Jesus' notoriety? Were they missing something concerning Jesus, something everyone else seemed aware of?

Relationships are precious, priceless assets. But when misunderstandings arise, these bonds can become an immense source of grief. Christ displayed a mastery of relationships, especially with Mary and the rest of His family who seemed unable to grasp the urgency of His time schedule. Operating within the framework of God's will and timing, Jesus always acted in *perfect unity* with the Father.

Take, for instance, the events surrounding the Feast of Tabernacles or Booths. Held on the fifteenth day of Tishri, the seventh month of the Jewish calendar, the feast commemorated the period when the Israelites dwelled in tents as they wandered for forty years in the wilderness. This annual fall festival took place during the final grain harvest of the year. As God Himself had called the observance, every Jewish male was therefore required to attend this joyous celebration.

"Now the feast of the Jews, the Feast of Tabernacles, was at hand. His brothers therefore said to Him, 'Depart from here, and go into Judea, that Your disciples also may behold Your works which You are doing. . . .' For not even His brothers were believing in Him." (John 7:2, 3)

As in any normal family, members have an unparalleled opportunity to examine each other's behavior. They had eaten with Jesus, slept in the same house, and observed every facet of His daily life. This afforded them ample time to become fully acquainted with His temperament and attitudes and also to scrutinize the reaction of others toward Him. *Jesus never sinned.* That alone should have provided insight into His unique character. And yet, as noted in the preceding verses, His brothers didn't understand He was the Son of God, their long-awaited Messiah.

Furthermore, they were obviously uninformed about the Sanhedrin's simmering caldron of hostility toward Jesus.

Since Jesus had dared to heal the sick on the Sabbath, those in desperate need had sought Him out, while the religious leaders perceived Him increasingly as a serious threat.

Thus His earthly brothers suggested that Jesus rush to the feast, making a grand entrance. Verse 4 of the seventh chapter of John reads, "Depart from here, and go into Judea, that Your disciples also may behold Your works which You are doing. For no one does anything in secret, when he himself hopes to be *known* publicly. If you do these things, show Yourself to the world."

Oblivious to the existing danger, Jesus' family was ready to leave for the feast. Attempting to stress the importance of *heavenly timing*, Jesus replied, "My time is not yet at hand, but your time is always opportune." (John 7:6) His family remained completely out of tune not only with His purpose for coming to earth but also His modus operandi. Jesus couldn't risk blazing into town trailed by an excessive entourage of followers.

Has your own family misunderstood your ministry or methods? Those closest to us are at times the last ones to recognize our talents as we move forward to fulfill our aspirations. Perhaps they can't be objective enough to view us as *real people* who have particular gifts and a distinct calling in life. But Jesus can identify with this form of grief.

At any rate, Jesus could not allow those who appeared incapable of discerning His ministry to dictate His actions. He arrived at the feast in the Father's time and in the Father's prescribed way. On the last day of the feast, the day of the Great Hallelujah, Jesus shouted, "If any man is thirsty, let him come to Me and drink." (John 7:37) His voice resounded within the temple walls as the priest poured the water, meant to symbolize God's Spirit being poured out on all men. The temple itself was filled with luminance signifying God's light.

Jesus Christ—Lamb of God, Savior of all, Light of the world, the Source of everlasting water for thirsty souls— is indeed the fulfillment of all feasts. He is the very reason they were instituted. As cited previously, Jesus stood in the temple and declared just that. Yet, sadly, neither Jesus' earthly family nor the religious leaders understood Him.

Jesus' half-brothers might have sought to align them-selves with Him because they had witnessed His miracles and heard His unusual message. They may have wanted to impress others by their association with this gifted and charismatic man. But, at that point, leaving everything behind to follow Jesus didn't interest them.

True identity with Christ requires bearing one's own cross of suffering. Later, James and Jude would become believers after being present in the Upper Room follow-ing Christ's Resurrection. Their New Testament epistles attest to all they had witnessed.*

During Christ's lifetime, the symbolic meaning of the feast was only partially fulfilled. Someday in the future the *final harvest,* which Jeremiah predicted, will take place. "I [God] will gather them out of all the lands to which I have driven them in My anger, in My wrath, in great in-dignation; and I will bring them back to this place and make them dwell in safety." (Jeremiah 32:37) One day the nation of Israel will ultimately look upon Jesus as their Messiah.

Until then we as Christians will continue to experience grief. We will be misunderstood, maligned, and mali-

---

*Warren W. Wiersbe, *Bible Exposition Commentary,* Vol. 2, Victor Books Publishing, 1989, p. 334.

ciously attacked for following God instead of the dictates of men and women. Yet we can draw comfort from the knowledge that Jesus has gone ahead of us, that He views us compassionately, and that He will provide the strength we need to keep moving forward.

One facet of the story of the wedding at Cana is Jesus' relationship with His earthly mother Mary. The bride and groom had run short of wine at their wedding party and Mary came to Jesus for assistance. Jesus answered her, "My hour has not come." (John 2:4) This is not a rebuke but a statement of fact. Yet Mary knew Jesus' heart and counted on His rescue. Rather than argue the matter, she simply instructed the servants to obey His directions.

Has your own family of origin challenged or questioned your every move? Because of that, have you perhaps allowed a dream to wither and die on the vine of your own heart? As you look back to your childhood and consider the blueprint you envisioned for adulthood, what grieves you? Have you forgiven those who altered your picture-perfect layout of life? If not, are you willing to do it now, in order to gain the necessary momentum to move ahead?

On the other hand, there may have been those who encouraged you to accelerate forward, risking everything to fulfill the impossible. It is imperative that we remember those who bolstered our ego as we stood at a critical junction, realizing the directional signs posted were, for whatever reason, unintelligible to us.

When our oldest son was four years old he disappeared one afternoon. Knowing that a new tract of homes was being constructed at the edge of our own housing development, I began searching for him there. There he stood, overlooking the footings, concrete, and rebar being prepared for the foundation of these modern dwellings. When

I inquired as to whether he had been bothering the work crew, one man answered, "No, but he sure asks a lot of questions!"

Kevin prattled on and on that day, describing all the things he had seen and explaining why the men proceeded in a certain way. His fascination with building things, as well as taking them apart to find out how they worked, seemed to take flight after that experience.

A short time later he and my husband, who has degrees in engineering, finance, and real estate, began building houses out of Lego blocks. These works of art remained on the coffee table until father and son had a desire to recycle the assembled blocks and begin anew. After years of drafting, and encouragement from a professor in this field, Kevin graduated with a degree in construction management. A successful assistant project manager, he and Karin have been married five years.

What would have happened if my husband hadn't taken time to nurture our son's little nucleus of interest? And what might have taken place if a Christian physician, Dr. David Messenger, who is now with the Lord, hadn't helped us get beyond our child's early hyperactivity and allergy attacks? Kevin might never have known the sense of accomplishment that comes from realizing your God-given talents.

Our second son, Jeff, expressed an interest in theology at an early age. Many of our after-school discussions, which centered on biblical issues, resulted in informative and well-documented reports he composed for school assignments. As he grew physically, his appetite for every book in my library also increased. Over the years he acquired his own fine library, taught junior high kids, and eventually completed his master's degree in biblical studies.

One Mother's Day I received a beautiful card from Jeff in which he thanked me for not only fostering his desire to learn but also for all those special conversations. How honored I am to have been there to plant the seeds of promise that God nurtured to maturity!

At only five years of age our daughter Bridget grabbed the shampoo bottle out of my hand and adamantly announced that she would wash her own hair. Throughout her early school years she maintained that her dream was to be a beautician. While other kids her age might have been bored watching their mother get a haircut, Bridget took note of every detail. Upon graduating from high school *she* enrolled in a nearby beauty school, and *my husband and I* soon became her weekly volunteers for cuts, perms, and color treatments. My first perm took eight agonizing hours!

Proudly we accompanied her to the cosmetology exam, and we even surprised her with her first pair of expensive shears. As her career has taken off, Bridget has managed to incorporate other natural skills into this occupation. She listens attentively to what her customers want, comforts friends in need, and encourages others with gentle words. With the hopes of someday owning her own salon, she returned to college a few years ago to obtain her management degree.

Lest you conclude that my husband and I did everything right, and become grief-stricken about your own parenting, let me assure you that we also bungled through with an abundance of horrendous mistakes. Yet God wiped away our tears as we continued to pray for the strong guidance of His written Word and relied heavily on His rescues throughout our children's formative years. Many times He scooped us off the floor where we knelt in utter defeat and despair, seeking His wisdom. But He never failed us!

Have your own dreams been relegated to a moldy old attic room, stuffed in a box marked "Storage," and scattered askew with other forgotten memories?

Consider Jack, a man in his late seventies. About thirty years ago Jack showed me an artist's palette and set of oil paints that lay nearly hidden in a cobwebbed corner of his basement work area. "I'm going to paint something one of these days," he asserted.

"Good, I'd love to see the finished project," I responded. Sadly, over three decades have passed and those oil pigments have dried up before they could ever splash across a canvas.

Much of our grief in life can be traced to those who gave us "burnt cookies." These people have either failed to affirm us or to nurture those brilliant, unrealized sketches that rattled around in our heads. Experience has shown that most of us can recall these incidents with amazing clarity.

Jack, the would-be van Gogh, grew up during the Depression. There wasn't time for personal aspirations; everyone had slipped into a survival mode. However, if he had been encouraged early on, there's no telling what he might have accomplished as he is an artistic and creative person with a great deal of patience. He has managed to cultivate other people's aspirations and that alone is a notable contribution to this world.

Perhaps the risk of failure loomed as large for Jack as it does for others and the prerecorded messages of hopelessness still resound within their minds. Perhaps like the servicemen of World War II who bought into Tokyo Rose's morale-defeating messages, you're giving way to the false propaganda of Satan.

Know that Christ never allowed the obstacles that confronted His ministry to deter His feet from the path of purpose. We can't afford to, either. Before you succumb to debilitating grief, reflect on these encouraging words God spoke to Jeremiah: "'For I know the plans that I have for you,' declares the LORD, 'plans for welfare and not for calamity to give you a future and a hope. Then you will call upon Me and come and pray to Me, and I will listen to you.'" (Jeremiah 29:11, 12)

Whether or not someone in your past took the time to nurture your inner longings, *God is here today*! And He's still saying that He has a custom-designed strategy for your life. No matter how buried your dreams, and regardless of your present circumstances, God still has a plan!

Consider those who long for children and whom the medical profession has sadly labeled *infertile*. If the previous paragraphs concerning my children were painful for you to read, I am truly sorry. Having lost a baby, I do understand this kind of grief.

Your personal goal may be to have a child, but God's primary objective for you is *wholeness in Him*. When I say *seek peace in His Word*, it isn't meant in any way to minimize your grief or patronize the problem. It's simply the truth!

Although Sarah may be the first childless woman who is mentioned in the Bible, let's consider Hannah, whose story is recorded for us in the first chapter of the first book of Samuel. To begin, Hannah's husband Elkanah had two wives. Now that's a sorry situation already! Of course, the other wife, Peninnah, had many sons and daughters. This rival would provoke and irritate Hannah year after year because "the Lord had closed her womb." (1 Samuel

1:1-28)

Remember, *nothing that happens to us is out of the view of God or takes place without His knowledge and consent*. Hannah became so distressed that she quit eating and drinking. Elkanah's response might be considered typical male insight. He reminded Hannah that he, her husband, was certainly "better to her than ten sons."

At this point Hannah's capabilities became restricted to praying and bitterly weeping over the grief of her childless state. Finally, in utter desperation, she began to bargain with God, promising the Lord that if He would give her a child she would dedicate him totally to God's service.

Seated by the doorpost of the temple, Eli the priest watched Hannah pray but he didn't hear her words. Instead, he just saw her mouth moving and no sounds coming forth from the well of grief stored in her heart. Eli concluded that Hannah must be drunk. Thus he consoled her by saying, "How long will you make yourself drunk?" Isn't anyone going to understand this poor woman?

When Hannah finally convinces Eli of her plight, Eli calls God's blessing down on her. Hannah then leaves the temple accompanied by her husband, with hope in her heart and a smile on her face. Perhaps this was Elkanah's last straw, too. At any rate, the Word says that they had relations "and the Lord remembered her." Ultimately, Hannah did deliver precious Samuel to Eli for service at the temple and God blessed her with three more sons and two daughters. (1 Samuel 2:21) Samuel went on to become a prophet of the Lord.

Did Hannah's bargain with God induce Him to answer the prayer? No, because God knew all along that Samuel would be born. However, this petition did benefit Hannah in four ways. First, her bargain prepared her heart for God's miracle. She was able to leave the weight of her grief in God's hands so that she could get on with her life. Thus Hannah could appreciate the utter magnitude of the miracle God performed for her. Lastly, she was faithful to her promise to render the child back to God, in spite of the fact that her mother's heart ached to keep him. The Lord rewarded her devotion by generously giving Hannah more children.

Fortunately, in these times, there are many qualified groups assisting those who experience this exceptional grief of the soul.* Perhaps by reaching out to others in your church family who suffer such grief, God will touch and heal the wound in your heart.

Another source of grief are the "wars and rumors of wars" that Jesus warned would preclude the great tribulation period during the final days of the world as we know it. Chapter 24 of Matthew's Gospel describes this time: "For nation will rise against nation, and kingdom against kingdom, and in various places there will be famines and earthquakes. But all these things are *merely* the beginning of birth pangs." (Matthew 24:7, 8)

Jesus continues in this account to describe the chronology of events. What isn't mentioned are the children for whom war is a daily occurrence and peace only a pipedream. A newspaper page filled with drawings by the children of Bosnia demonstrates aptly how they view their world. Gone are the shapes of neat little homes with families warmly snuggled inside. Instead the children's crayons illustrate vivid, blood-red scenes of war, bombs

---

* The Stepping Stones Ministry of the Central Christian Church, Wichita, Kansas, publishes a newsletter for infertile couples and also has a reading list available on request. For more information, write the ministry at 2900 N. Rock Road, Wichita, KS 67226-1198. See Bibliography for helpful reading material on this subject.

destroying homes, dragons that breathe fire upon unsuspecting victims, and bullet-riddled dead bodies strewn in the streets of a once glorious city. Childhood isn't supposed to be this way!

While finishing this chapter, word came that Nancy, a dear friend of mine, had died of cancer. My grief is fresh and unexpressed. Shock and disbelief are creeping ever so slowly into my soul, like a night mist.

All that consoles me is that that she'll be "home for Christmas," her favorite time of year. For Years we exchanged lovely handmade ornaments, a wonderful tradition of friendship. As I place these delicate decorations on the tree this year, they will assume an even more treasured place in my heart.

But along with thoughts of her favorite things, one of her own "burnt cookie" experiences came to mind. Once a stack of her grandmother's letters was inadvertently thrown away. Losing this visible token of love broke Nancy's heart because this correspondence was all she had left of someone who had believed in her. Now she and her granny are together again, safe in the arms of Jesus. Nancy has taken that trunk of grief and placed it gently at her Savior's nail-pierced feet.

In tribute to my precious friend, who continued to trust and not ask "Why, Lord?", here is a verse that I know she loved and lived by. "My frame was not hidden from you when I was made in the secret place. When I was woven together in the depths of the earth, your eyes saw my unformed body. All the days ordained for me were written in your book before one of them came to be." (Psalm 139:15, 16, NIV)

The date is fixed in time. If *you* died tonight, do you know where you would spend eternity? Nancy did!

8

Satchels of Heart Strength

And He said to them, "Why are you troubled, and why do doubts arise in your hearts?" (Luke 24:38)

While Jesus walked with Cleopas and the other man on their way to Emmaus, He fully explained the Scriptures to them. Later, their sandals kicking up clouds of red-brown dust, the two travelers recounted the day's events as they hurried back down the road toward Jerusalem. Christ had suddenly vanished from sight, yet His words lingered on. "Were not our hearts burning within us while He was speaking to us on the road, while He was explaining the Scriptures to us?" (Luke 24:32) Finally they understood the big picture, the whole story, and they couldn't wait to share it all with the disciples.

They found the eleven, and the others who were with them, in the Upper Room, deeply involved in their grief. Like the two on their way to Emmaus, these followers of Christ had determined that if Jesus would finally *redeem* Israel, then He must become their king by ruling over the Romans who oppressed them. Somehow, they had accepted a plan that precluded a *suffering and dying savior.*

Hadn't they heard His words over and over? Jesus had plainly announced to the Jews, "For this reason the Father loves Me, because I lay down My life that I may take it again. No one has taken it away from Me, but I lay it down on My own initiative. I have authority to lay it down, and I have authority to take it up again." (John 10:17, 18)

Peter had been in Bethany when Jesus had called a very dead Lazarus out of the tomb and restored him to life. Surely he must have heard the Lord tell Martha that He was "the resurrection and the life. . . ." (John 11:25) Wouldn't it be reasonable to assume that Christ meant what He said about *having the authority to raise Himself from the dead*? But Peter might have been saying to himself, "Wait, this is a whole new concept. Nobody's ever done things like this before! Give me time to understand."

Christ had already stamped Peter's account "paid in full." In a little while they would talk and get their relationship back on track. But for now the urgent matter at hand was the disciples' state of despondency. *Doubt and fear*, that helpless and hopeless condition familiar to all grieving persons, had bored its way into their hearts.

Suddenly Jesus stood in their midst. He read the futility that streaked across their mourning brows and then He showed them His hands and feet. The scars from His crucifixion had not been erased during the Resurrection. They were plain to see. Now anyone and everyone could exercise the option for a clean slate, unburdened by the weight of sin, grief, and guilt. But before they could enter His kingdom, they had to be willing to *accept Him on His terms*, as Messiah, Lord, and Savior. As the One who had shed His precious blood for all humankind.

After displaying the indelible marks, the searing brand of love borne in their behalf, Jesus surprised them by asking if they had anything to eat. They responded by giving Him a piece of broiled fish. "Then He opened their minds to understand the Scriptures." (Luke 24:45)

Peter's last glimpse of Jesus had taken place in the courtyard of the high priest. What a horrible, frightful night! First, in the Garden of Gethsemane, the Lord had admonished Peter and the others, "Pray that you may not enter into temptation." (Luke 22:40) Instead, their grief and sorrow over the dinner conversation, in which Jesus had announced that He must die, had caused them to fall into the complete mental escape that sleep affords. How Peter wished he had heeded the Lord's words! But the ensuing facts of the evening could not be relived. Jesus had been arrested, the cock had crowed, and Peter had denied the Lord not once but *three times*.

Peter desired to put it all behind him, but the self-loathing of his actions gnawed at him like a ravenous rodent. Surely the other disciples knew about his shameful actions, and probably wondered how he could face Jesus. Peter turned his gaze downward, toward well-worn sandals.

But the Lord *had* returned, and Peter could not resist those incredible, magnetic eyes filled not only with light but also *love*. Did Peter wrestle silently within himself? Did he wonder what price he would have to pay for his cowardly deed? We can only guess, but at his core Peter undoubtedly longed to hear his Lord's voice again, and to hear the truth of Scripture poured forth with the welcome nectar of promise.

On the night when the disciples had shared the last Passover with Jesus, they had become exhilarated at the prospect of being included in His Kingdom. In fact, they had even argued about who should have the best positions within that majestic realm. Consequently, when Jesus began relating the excruciating reality that *suffering and death* would precede this domain, they simply tuned it out. Aren't we just the same? How easy it is to practice selective emotional deafness when unpleasant, frightening, or complex problems arise.

Yet for Peter to accept a major role in spreading the Gospel, complete fellowship had to be reestablished between Jesus and himself. Peter, after all, would take the *Good News* to the Jews.

Names are extremely important within Middle Eastern cultures as they are chosen to denote one's character. When Jesus had first called Simon to follow Him, He renamed him Peter, meaning "a stone." As long as Peter relied on the Lord, he would have that needed strength of character.

Just prior to their departure from the Passover meal, Jesus divulged key information to Peter. Within that warning, which Jesus addressed to Peter, He reverted back to the name of his birth. "Simon, Simon, behold, Satan has demanded *permission* to sift you like wheat; but I have prayed for you, that your faith may not fail; and you, when once you have turned again, strengthen your brothers." (Luke 22:31, 32) Did Peter miss Jesus' subtle but critical prophecy? Did Peter remember Jesus' words of restoration?

That night in the Garden of Gethsemane Peter overreacted when the guards came to seize Christ. In this burst of thoughtless enthusiasm, while attempting to *protect* Jesus, he inadvertently cut off Malchus's ear. Before this incident could escalate, Jesus replaced the ear and healed the wound of the high priest's slave. This miracle not only diffused the mounting tensions but also insured that Peter's life was spared.

Peter's hot-headed response was unnecessary. When the

Roman cohort, chief priests, and Pharisees came seeking "Jesus of Nazareth" with their torches and weapons, Jesus simply answered, "*I am*," (John 18:6) and they fell to the ground. Jesus used *God's eternal name*, for Jesus is God. Just the power of Christ's spoken words going out across this mob had completely overtaken them. Jesus could have called thousands of angels to assist Him, but He chose to drink the cup of suffering that would redeem us. How could Peter have ever doubted that he would be forgiven?

The time for restoration had arrived and Jesus gave these fishermen a catch they would never forget. As He reached out to Peter again, He said, "Simon, *son* of John, do you love Me more than these?" That's what it all gets down to. *God equates love with obedience.* Three times Jesus asks this question, attempting to get Peter to use the word *agape*, a divine and self-sacrificing love, the kind of love Jesus has shown for him. (John 21:15) Yet each time Peter uses instead the word *phileo*, a term of brotherly affection. (John 21:16, 17) Was Peter terrified to admit the true depth of his love for Christ, lest he fail Him again?*

Jesus understands Peter's heart and renews his call back into service: "Tend My sheep," He says, and then adds, "Follow Me!" (John 21: 17, 19) Just as Peter denied Christ publicly three times, Jesus has allowed him to affirm Him three times. Christ does not doubt Peter's leadership abilities and neither should the other disciples.

The love Jesus has for Peter, as for all of us, is as strong when we're *lost* as when we're *found*. Now Peter could lay aside his grief-filled grip and exchange it for a satchel of strength. He had received forgiveness from the risen Christ. Later he would write two New Testament epistles,

---

*Warren W. Wiersbe, *Bible Exposition Commentary*, vol. 1, Victor Books, 1989, p. 398.

First and Second Peter, that explain the true depth of God's mercy. Peter's faith had been singed at the campfire and now was restored by love to wholeness. Now only death—his own, as a martyr—would restrain Peter from telling the entire story to everyone he met.

Jesus understood about broken hearts. In the previous chapter the failure of Jesus' earthly family to understand His divine time schedule was discussed. When Jesus returned to Nazareth, they even accused Jesus of having lost His mind: ". . .and the multitude gathered again, to such an extent that they could not even eat a meal. And when His own people heard *of this*, they went out to take custody of Him; for they were saying, 'He has lost His senses.'" (Mark 3:20, 21)

Jesus' family, like the entourage of a celebrity today, was trying to rewrite their shining star's agenda. Yet as long as people were receptive to hearing the *words of truth*, Jesus didn't allow anything to deter Him from reaching and mending their shattered lives. Are we just as determined to get out the Gospel? Are we willing to go without food, sleep, and even shelter, as Jesus did, so that the lives of others will be forever altered by the only words that can alleviate their grief?

There existed a time when Paul, the apostle, would have answered that question with a definite and resounding no! Paul had not only been present at the stoning of Stephen, but he was in "hearty agreement" (Acts 8:1) with the heinous act. Even the sight of Stephen's face, "like the face of an angel" (Acts 6:15) before he died, had no seeming effect on Saul, as he was called then. Did Saul consider what *power* could motivate Stephen to forgive the very people who were killing him, while they were performing this act of cruelty?

Saul's presence at Stephen's stoning is clearly recorded in the Bible (Acts 7:58): "And when they had driven him out of the city, they *began* stoning *him*, and the witnesses laid aside their robes at the feet of a young man named Saul." Could he have been any closer to the scene of the crime?

Furthermore, following Stephen's death the persecution of Christians intensified, threatening to annihilate the newborn church. The grief endured by those who were called to be uprooted and relocated from their homes and families during this persecution is beyond imagination. Except for the apostles, the believers became scattered throughout Judea and Samaria to spread the Word to new locations.

Saul's role in the continued onslaught of Christians is graphically depicted: "But Saul *began* ravaging the church, entering house after house; and dragging off men and women, he would put them in prison." (Acts 8:3) Seeking to capture even those who had fled his grasp, Saul's heart brimmed with murderous threats. He asked the high priest "for letters from him to the synagogues at Damascus, so that if he found any belonging to the Way, both men and women, he might bring them bound to Jerusalem." (Acts 9:2)

This action would change his life forever. On his way to Damascus Saul was blinded by a brilliant light from heaven. Falling to the ground, he heard a voice and, when he asked who it was, the voice answered, "Saul, Saul, why are you persecuting Me? . . .I am Jesus whom you are persecuting." (Acts 9:4-5) Then the voice directed him to enter the city where he would then be given further instructions. Those who were with him led him by the hand. For three days Saul remained sightless and without food or drink. Pain has a way of dispelling spiritual darkness.

Enter a disciple of the Lord named Ananias. God in a dream had told Saul that this same man, Ananias, would lay his hands on him and his vision would be restored. However, Saul's reputation as a persecutor of the church had preceded him. Ananias, wanting no part of this deal, was probably asking God, respectfully, "What part of *no* don't You understand?"

The Lord gave Ananias these instructions: "Go, for he is a chosen instrument of Mine, to bear My name before the Gentiles and kings and the sons of Israel; for I will show him how much he must suffer for My name's sake." (Acts 9:15, 16) Perhaps hearing that Saul was now going to suffer provided the enticement Ananias required to obey the Lord. At any rate, he did lay hands on Saul and explained who it was that had blinded him. Only a personal encounter with the risen Christ caused Saul to accept finally that Jesus was the Son of God and to receive the Holy Spirit.

The rushing tide of hatred turned. As soon as Saul began preaching the Gospel in the synagogues, the Jews who sent him there to kill the Christians began plotting *his* own murder. When he tried to convince the disciples of his conversion, they remained terrified of him. There was no one from his old life Saul could turn to, and no one from his new life willing to risk accepting him. Have you ever felt that isolated?

On the night I made my Christian confession of faith and accepted the Lord as my Savior, I experienced both the loftiest and most devastating emotions of my life. Wanting to announce my "new life," I called a relative to share the incredible revelation that Christ had given me wholeness. Instead of sharing in my jubilation, she reacted by giving me a ration of grief that wouldn't quit.

Here I had just declared my involvement in the greatest love relationship of my life and this person didn't get it! In that moment, I felt compelled to make the same decision as Paul. No matter what I surrendered, it couldn't compare with knowing Christ. I would continue to move forward and not look back, and I would pray for those who chose not to follow Him. Over twenty years later, I'm still trusting, leaning, and obeying because of His strength, not mine.

Paul and Peter both embraced Christ's message with all their hearts, and not only for their future but for their present. Their personal encounters with the risen Christ determined how the rest of their lives would be spent. Both of these apostles were martyred for their faith, and then they were ushered into paradise by the One they served so faithfully. Are you so convinced of the truth of the Gospel message that it has become the standard by which you live? Are you secure with the knowledge of your own eternal destination?

A. Wetherell Johnson, founder of the Bible Study Fellowship, knew with certainty whom she served. Like Paul, however, she hadn't always known the truth. Although she had grown up in a Christian home, she had never made a personal commitment to Him. While in her early twenties she had even been an agnostic. Yet slowly God drew her to Himself.

In comparison with the people she knew to be *good*, she considered herself *unworthy*. Then there was the problem of *unconfessed sin in her life*, which she acknowledged and yet refused to surrender to the Lord. In time she began to pity those in her family who believed in what she termed "biblical myths." *

---

*A. Wetherell Johnson, *Created for Commitment*, Tyndale House Publishers, 1982, pp. 30-31.

Educated during her early years in England, Johnson later settled in France where she became acquainted with professors and journalists from many European countries. Their philosophies and politics not only intrigued her but drew her into the sophisticated secular world she hadn't experienced before. Studying the works of Friedrich Nietzsche, Jean Jacques Rousseau, and Voltaire drew her away from the belief system of her Christian home. Once the erosion of truth had taken place, she recalls feeling like a house whose foundation has cracked and crumbled until it is beyond repair.

Accompanying this deepening awareness of despair and hopelessness was her stubborn refusal to respond to the Lord's clear call. Her mother prayed for her, while her father, who was completely unaware of this inner struggle, insisted she attend a business school and prepare for her future. After finishing her studies, she became a registrar for a public high school.

Yet nothing alleviated her growing inward sense of desperation and meaninglessness. Unable to bear this confusion any longer, she prayed one evening in the confines of her locked bedroom. "God, if there be a God, if You will give me some philosophy that makes reasonable sense to me, I will commit myself to follow it." *

While her mind struggled over philosophical choices, a verse of Scripture wove its way back from her childhood: "He who believes in Him is not judged; he who does not believe has been judged already, because he has not believed in the name of the only begotten Son of God." (John 3:18) Like the serpentine tail of a kite, God's Word jerked and pulled her from the lies until she at last returned to the point of truth.

Johnson's struggle had been whether or not she could

*Ibid., p. 33.

accept Jesus as the Son of God. She had discounted this truth when she refused to accept the *virgin birth*. Now as suddenly as Paul had seen God's blinding light of truth, so did she. Her dilemma resolved, she fell on her knees and worshiped Him as Savior and Lord.

From that time on, God used her life to build a ministry that would bring tens of thousands of others to Him as they studied His Word through the Bible Study Fellowship. It was my privilege to attend for five years as a student and then to go on and teach for an additional five years in this special organization. Although A. Wetherell Johnson has gone home to be with her wondrous Lord, the Bible study she began continues to flourish.

Another life that has left an indelible imprint on my heart and soul is that of Kay Arthur, cofounder of Precept Ministries. Even now as I listen to her testimony on tape, it is difficult to reconcile the account of her life apart from Christ with the one she lives today.

As the mother of two young sons, Arthur found herself overwhelmed by the sense that something was desperately missing. On the outside everything looked fine: a nice husband, beautiful home, and wonderful family. She had a mink, money, and even the possibility of a modeling career. Yet a terrible emptiness consumed her soul.

One evening, which she can vividly recall, she and her husband argued and in a rage she hurled her wedding rings at him. Later, she left home with their sons and went to look, in her words, for someone who would love her unconditionally. With deep regret she readily admits throwing off all the teaching that had been instilled in her by her parents. In her words she became "an immoral woman," and the weight of this sin dragged her down.*

*"My Story" (cassette tape), Kay Arthur's testimony, Precept Ministries, P.O. Box 182218. Chattanooga, TN 37422-7218.

But God's rescue was already in progress. Invited by a Christian man to a party at his home, Arthur met honest people who told her what she needed. When a guest advised, "Kay, why don't you quit telling God what you want and tell Him Jesus Christ is all you need," Arthur had a flippant answer. She replied, "Jesus is not all I need. I need a husband, a. . ." and proceeded to deliver a long list. She then threw her mink over her shoulder and went home.

But, she couldn't forget the words they had spoken. Finally, she sunk down beside her bed and begged God to give her *true peace*. He obliged by giving her *the Prince of Peace.*

God's timing in her life was perfect, as always. When the husband she had left committed suicide by hanging himself, only God's strength brought her through. Only God's power could ease her burden of guilt and mend her shattered heart. Since then Kay Arthur has dedicated her life to teaching people how to study God's Word inductively, so they can know the truth for themselves.

We have seen that Jesus' own heart was broken by the actions of different people. His earthly family didn't understand His timing, purpose, or level of commitment to the Father. His disciple, Judas Iscariot, betrayed Him. Peter denied knowing Him three times. Finally, the rest of the disciples fled at His hour of greatest need, at the hour He was to die for them on Calvary. Yet Jesus came back to restore their faith, give them hope, and calm the consuming grief in their hearts.

Is your own heart troubled? Are you ready to lay down your own suitcase full of grief and accept the gift of completeness He now offers?

9

Kicking that Knapsack of Grief

For where two or three have gathered together in My name, there I am in their midst. (Matthew 18:20)

The tacky web of untouched grief is taut and constricting. Our hands may tear and tug at its thin strands, hoping to transport ourselves quickly to freedom, while our thought powers become sapped from devising a plan of escape. No longer will our emotions become titillated at the thought of taking part in joyful activities. Instead, all focus in our universe is pinpointed on that blip in time when the physicality of grief swallowed up our last free breath and replaced it with an ache that can only be described as a spiritual vacuum. However, it is within this dark dungeon of seeming abandonment that God Himself has promised to meet us and make His presence known.

Although Jesus set this verse of Scripture within the framework of His teaching on forgiveness, it definitely applies to untouched grief. For it is when the pain of loss has decimated our spirits, as a late autumn wind strips the golden boughs of maples, that we must set claim to the strong foundation of Jesus Christ. *Know that our prayers can propel us back into His very presence and equip us to release the agony that consumes our souls.*

Those who continue to be supported by the One who is the very rock of our faith, Jesus Christ, can withstand even the gale force winds of grief. When we understand that prayer itself is our strongest weapon against such instability, we can press forward. Therefore, we must perceive the *process and priorities of prayer.*

Prayer establishes our sense of *communication with our Creator.* When Adam and Eve inhabited the Garden of Eden, we know that God sought them out. "And they heard the sound of the LORD God walking in the garden in the cool of the day, and the man and his wife hid themselves from the presence of the LORD God among the trees of the garden. Then the LORD God called to the man, and said to him, 'Where are you?'" (Genesis 3:8, 9)

The problem is that many times God must seek us out and ask that same question, "Where are you?" He is cognizant that we certainly aren't where we belong. As God searched the garden for Adam and Eve, who had sinned and needed restoration to fellowship with Him, He also endeavors to reveal Himself as our only source of sustenance. Remember that although *grief is not sin*, it does produce a similar sense of isolation. This is partly because we assume that if God gives only *good gifts*, then pain and suffering can't be His will for us.

However, out of His love for us our Father allows things to happen that are ultimately going to promote our spiritual growth and dependence on Him. The old adage, "Take this medicine, it's good for you," does not apply here. Instead, God says, "Come, let Me show you that I will walk *with you* through this pain and agony until it doesn't hurt anymore because I love you with a greater love than you will ever know."

Second, as out of focus as our lives might seem, while we're grieving, *prayer* brings it all back into clear view, renewing our perspective. Before He went to the cross, Jesus prayed for His disciples' protection: "I have given them Thy word; and the world has hated them, because they are not of the world, even as I am not of the world. I do not ask Thee to take them out of the world, but to keep them from the evil *one*." (John 17:14, 15) Christ knew that He was about to leave the disciples in the hands of the very people who were about to crucify Him. It grieved Him to depart physically from those He loved and trained, His precious flock of lambs who would be slaughtered for the cause of the Gospel.

Jesus' disciples were not of this world; someday they would join Him in the Kingdom. This leads to another major point: Our own suffering is for the most part a surprise event. Therefore, the third thing required is that we undergird our lives with *consistent prayer*. Even if we might anticipate someone's death, as in the case of a physician's diagnosis as terminal, we still aren't privy to the exact moment when the full weight of grief will overtake us.

But Jesus *knew* exactly what was going to transpire and He still chose to go to the cross for us. As Christ sought to protect His disciples from those who came to arrest Him in the Garden of Gethsemane, He willingly stepped forward and identified Himself. We read this account from John's Gospel: "Jesus therefore, knowing all the things that were coming upon Him, went forth, and said to them, 'Whom do you seek?'" (John 18:4)

While sharing their last Passover meal, prior to their departure for the Garden of Gethsemane, Jesus had also warned the disciples, "Truly, truly, I say to you, that one of you will betray Me." (John 13:20) Yet He went to the appointed place of betrayal and prayed diligently because it was vitally important that He be absolutely in tune with *the Father's will and timing*. Throughout His ministry Jesus had been taunted and tempted by Satan to *change the plan*. Therefore, these last petitions Christ would offer to the Father would be the most critical of all.

"And when He arrived at the place, He said to them, 'Pray that you may not enter into temptation.'" (Luke 22:40) Jesus wanted to warn the disciples that the evil one lurked about, hoping to rob them of both His words and works that had convinced them that He truly was the Son of God. If Satan could plunder their precious belief in the Messiah, the disciples would have no hope for a solution to their grief. Therefore, Christ prayed so fervently for His disciples, and for all the imminent suffering ahead, that His sweat became like drops of blood and fell upon the ground. "An angel from heaven appeared to Him, strengthening Him" that He might get beyond this grief. (Luke 22:43, 44)

This then is the fourth point: We must pray that we not be strangled in the grips of *temptation*. Instead of giving way to the thoughts that invade our minds and are clearly contrary to the Word of God, we must reach out and grasp biblical truths. *Memorizing Scripture* is vitally important to our health and well-being. When grief has begun to erode our stability, we need to grab whatever is familiar—and true—and hold on for dear life.

King David, from whom the Messiah, Jesus Christ, was a direct descendant, habitually cried out to the Lord during his times of greatest sorrow. Reading through the Psalms assures us that David heeded the admonition of Scripture. Therefore, the fifth point is to "pray without ceasing." (Philippians 4:6, KJV)

Christ has shown us by His own example of prayer that it was indeed *constant*. Just as He sought to alert the disciples over 2,000 years ago, He warns each of us now that the days ahead will test us like never before. During His time on earth Jesus also prayed for all those who would live in the future.

We know that during the daylight hours Christ's time remained busy and hectic, like ours. In Luke's Gospel we read, "Now during the day He was teaching in the temple . . . ." (Luke 21:37a) Jesus prayed either in the early morning hours or in the late evening when the crowds of people would cease from following Him. ". . .But at evening He would go out and spend the night on the mount that is called Olivet. And all the people would get up early to come to Him in the temple to listen to Him." (Luke 21:37b-38)

As stated in a previous chapter, the Mount of Olives remained Christ's place of prayer. Jesus would actually spend the night on that mountain. The Greek word for night, *vu núx*, means "continuously through the night." The King James Version uses the word abode (the Greek word *aulízomai*) which in this context means "to live or lodge in fields or outdoors at night." Do you have a specific place for prayer?

Be wary of those who would tell you that Jesus lived anything other than the humble life of a suffering servant. He didn't even have a place to call home. His entire life was poured out in love for us, that we might learn by His blessed example how to endure in every trial. He stayed close to the Father because He and the Father are One. That is where we belong, not only when we want to celebrate something wonderful, but also when we are despairing from grief. The sixth point, therefore, is this: Prayer is *abiding*.

Jesus tenderly explained this unique relationship to His disciples once Judas Iscariot, the betrayer, had left the Passover dinner to put his evil plan in motion. His timing was and is always perfect: This special friendship with Jesus is only available to those who truly believe in Him. "After a little while the world will behold Me no more; but you *will* behold Me; because I live, you shall live also. In that day you shall know that I am in My Father, and you in Me, and I in you." (John 14:19, 20) Following this He expounded on God's meaning of abiding. "If anyone loves Me, he will keep My word; and My Father will love him, and We will come to him, and make Our abode with him." (John 14:23)

There it is again, that word *obedience*. Yet it is the key to all that God desires to give us, including His very presence, to see us through our times of grief. Have you stuffed all your pain inside a knapsack that you then throw across your back in the hopes of making it less visible to others? Guess what, it still shows! We can never *hide grief*, but we can *give it away* to the One who loves us enough to *bear it for us*.

When I was a small child I asked my grandfather what I should pray about. He instructed, "Only bother God for the big things." Although he meant well, this was terrible advice. From then on I tended to minimize each crisis, assuming I could handle it alone. Eventually, his words restrained me from crying out for assistance.

Has someone in your life, whether intentional or not, diminished the immensity of God's caring for you? Worry no more because Christ has given us a green light to His presence in prayer. "Come to Me, all who are weary and heavy-laden, and I will give you rest. Take My yoke upon you, and learn from Me, for I am gentle and humble in heart; and YOU SHALL FIND REST FOR YOUR SOULS. For My yoke is easy, and My load is light." (Matthew 11:28-30)

Are you ready yet to slip your arms out of that knapsack of grief and hand it to Him? Maybe you've grown so accustomed to carrying it that you can't even lift it up over your head. Or do you feel this burden is somehow warranted? Has someone interfered and decreased your worth to the point that you don't think you deserve to feel loved, protected, and cherished on a human level, let alone by the God of this universe? Such treatment is known as *emotional abuse.*

According to Andrew Vachss, attorney and author, "Emotional abuse is the systematic diminishment of another. It may be intentional or subconscious (or both), but it is always a course of conduct, not a single event."* Emotional abuse is like watching the undulating waves of the ocean erode the biggest rock until its smooth surface belies the rock's once distinct character.

Your Father in heaven would never treat you that way. In fact, He says you're worth everything. By the way, don't confuse emotional abuse with low self-esteem. Too much attention has already been focused on the issue of self-esteem, which in the end translates as a counterfeit of what God has to offer to us. *Remember, we can never conjure up a feeling of self-worth apart from Him.*

The issue of emotional abuse tears away at the wondrous and unique creation God made when He fashioned your form. No one has the right to take this from you. Allow Him to reach over gently and lift that grief-filled

*Andrew Vachss, "You Carry the Cure in Your Own Heart," *Parade* magazine, August 28, 1994, p. 4.

knapsack from your shoulders. Soon He will begin to heal the deep depressions caused from bearing a weight you were never designed to carry.

Jesus says that He desires to bless us: "If you then, being evil, know how to give good gifts to your children, how much more shall *your* heavenly Father give the Holy Spirit to those who ask Him?" (Luke 11:13) The reason Christ came to earth in the first place was to obtain access to the Father for us. We must *truly believe* that He is the Son of God, the Messiah, our propitiation for sin, and the *only way* to heaven. The seventh point on prayer is that *we can access the very throne of God* with our petitions. Yet even this unmerited favor to speak with our God is possible because of Christ.

How dishonest it would be then to consider coming before the throne, being confronted with God's holiness, without first forgiving those against whom we harbor anger or resentment! The eighth benefit of prayer is that it *allows us the opportunity of forgiveness*. We cannot possibly rid ourselves of grief if we allow it to infect our hearts. Christ admonished His disciples, "And whenever you stand praying, forgive, if you have anything against anyone; so that your Father also who is in heaven may forgive you your transgressions." (Mark 11:25)

Rest assured Jesus wasn't speaking about the *position of prayer*. Although within the Gospels we have accounts of Jesus kneeling and standing to pray, perhaps the prayer He said for us while hanging on the cross became His greatest. "Father, forgive them; for they do not know what they are doing." (Luke 23:34) In His own hour of greatest grief, Jesus forgave all those whose sins had placed Him there, and that includes all of us and those who have hurt us also. For Christ knew that if we attempted to live with an unforgiving spirit, that spirit would consume us.

The grief of holding onto yesterday and projecting more pain for tomorrow leaves us with absolutely nothing to grasp onto today. Who is your chief source of grief? A relative, a friend, your mate, your kids, your in-laws? Or is it God Himself? Do you harbor a secret anger that God has failed you in some way? Maybe you can't even whisper this truth in prayer because you're afraid He might strike you with lightning or something worse! He can take it. Just start with honesty and Jesus will meet you there.

There has to be an initial point of contact. When I asked some friends why they didn't go to church, they recited a list of people who "called themselves Christians" and yet had failed to show them real love. An incident occurred within one congregation during a true crisis in their lives. They perceived that since this group of individuals failed miserably to understand or display compassion that God Himself had also seemingly faltered in His ability to care.

Now these two people are in their late fifties. They have never forgiven either the members of that fellowship or their God. And have never approached the doorstep of a church again. One can only wonder how someone can reach such faulty conclusions. Why do they assume that if someone is a "true Christian" they should be able to meet all our needs? Sorry, only our Lord can do that! To blame God for the failings of His creation will never alleviate us of our responsibility to seek Him, serve Him, and love Him with all our hearts.

Is there someone against whom you harbor bitterness? Are you willing to allow our all-powerful God to heal this estrangement and rescue you from this grief-producing memory? Let God demonstrate His awesome power of forgiveness within you.

We must not request, however, His action in our life without being ready for the result. *Prayer indeed effects change*, and is the ninth point concerning petitions to God.

James, the earthly half-brother of our Lord, knew this to be true. He used an account from the life of Elijah the prophet to teach about prayer. "Therefore, confess your sins to one another, and pray for one another, so that you may be healed. The effective prayer of a righteous man can accomplish much. Elijah was a man with a nature like ours, and he prayed earnestly that it might not rain; and it did not rain on the earth for three years and six months. And he prayed again, and the sky poured rain, and the earth produced its fruit." (James 5:16-18)

Did you catch the fact that Elijah had a nature like ours? He had a need and he took it to God. How can we know what the Lord is prepared to do in any given situation? We will never be able to second-guess Him because He will answer our prayer in a unique way.

One night I was awakened out of a sound sleep and immediately I began to pray for our daughter. Unaware of any specific problem, my prayers took on an urgency as the hollow feeling within my stomach increased. I asked the Lord to "surround our daughter with angels." Within about a half-hour her boyfriend called to say they had been in a terrible car accident and my daughter had been taken to a nearby hospital.

Her injuries included a concussion, severe whiplash, and back injuries, scrapes, and bruises. Considering the nature of the accident—they had been rear-ended by an eighteen-wheeler and then propelled into two parked cars—it was a miracle that either of them survived.

Months of physical therapy followed for our daughter while her boyfriend sustained only a minor injury to his wrist.

Although I praised God for this amazing rescue, at the time I wasn't aware how incredible it had been. A few weeks later I received a call from the insurance company, representing the truck driver. After I finished giving the adjuster a statement as to injuries both passengers experienced, she asked a strange question on behalf of her client. "What happened to the man in the back seat? Our driver is terribly concerned that he didn't survive the crash!"

"There was no one in the back seat," I assured her. "However, I did ask God to surround her with angels!" In that moment I had my own confirmation. My God had roused me from sleep, prompted me to pray, and, in response to that prayer, He had sent an angel to protect them. Lest we forget, God dispatched an angel to deliver His servants, Daniel's three friends, from the fiery furnace. (Daniel 3:28)

Lastly, let us look again at the *pattern for prayer* that Christ gave us. The disciples had observed Jesus praying and asked Him to teach them how to pray. Jesus responded by giving them what we call the Lord's Prayer. "Our Father who art in heaven, Hallowed be Thy name. Thy kingdom come. Thy will be done, on earth as it is in heaven. Give us this day our daily bread. And forgive us our debts, as we also have forgiven our debtors. And do not lead us into temptation, but deliver us from evil. (For Thine is the kingdom, and the power, and the glory, forever. Amen.)" (Matthew 6:9-13)

Did Jesus intend for this to be their only prayer, repeated over and over? Remember, He had cautioned them not to use meaningless repetition as the Gentiles did. (Matthew 6:7) Instead, Jesus gave them the Lord's Prayer as a pattern because it contained all the elements of a good and perfect prayer: Adoration, Confession, Thanksgiving, and Supplication. By using the acrostic, ACTS, you can easily remember this format.

Our God is the only one who is worthy of *adoration,* so it is fitting that we approach Him with awe and wonder. We will never fully understand His attributes or His all-encompassing love for us.

As we *confess* our sins, we are enabled to come into His presence for prayer. Remember, He is absolutely holy. Before the Jewish priests could enter the temple, they had to perform an entire ritual of washing their bodies. Confession does for our soul what bathing accomplishes for our body. Confession also enables us to be more receptive to what the Lord will direct us to do since our minds are then free and clear.

Next, we must *thank* the Lord for all He has done for us. Why is this important? Think of it in human terms. Imagine if you asked a friend for another gift when you had never thanked her for the last one. How much more ungrateful this appears to the One who not only sustains our lives, but allows us to bring the Words of life to others!

Unfortunately, most people dash right into God's presence and begin with their supplications or needs. However, *supplications* are to be asked last, following our adoration, confession, and thanksgiving. God desires that our prayers be lifted up daily, from our hearts and with reverence for *who He is.* His response is to answer these petitions in a way that is best for us.

A simple prayer notebook is a helpful adjunct when becoming accustomed to this concept of prayer. It doesn't have to be fancy, a small three-ring binder will do, but it should include divider tabs for separating the categories. To get started, under the *Adoration* section write the different attributes of God. In the section of the things you wish to *Confess,* these need not be written but may include a few notes or key words. Another addition here might be the names of those who have harmed you. Keep in mind you can't remain angry with them if you're praying for them. Under the *Thanksgiving* section record the prayers that the Lord has already mightily answered, like saving my daughter from devastating damage in that car accident.

Finally, address the section we'll call *Prayer needs*. When my children were small they would leave their weekly requests on my "prayer chair" each Monday morning. Requests would include concerns about tests, teachers, and maybe a special reminder about some bully at school. Of course, as they grew up the prayers became more intense and for larger issues. It's comforting that even with all of them out of the house they still call and request prayer for specific needs. I pray for each family member in order: first my husband, and then each child according to the order in which God presented them to me. Then I pray for the extended family.

After this make as many sections as you need, but don't get too carried away or you'll become overwhelmed. One divider section could be for *Teachers and schools*, while another might be labeled *Pastor and elders*. Don't forget to pray for your pastor as his responsibilities and his need for protection from any evil influence that would hinder his ministry are tremendous. Another category I included in my notebook is *Government officials*. God says they are directly responsible to Him for all the decisions they make. Therefore, we had better pray that they make the right ones. If you don't want to trouble yourself making a notebook, such a resource can be purchased in most Christian bookstores.

More important that any notebook is that *prayer is God's transformer for our lives and the lives of others.* We can change nothing without Him. Will you allow Him to sit beside you and remove that heavy load of grief?

10

A Sarcophagus
of Suffering

*Truly, truly, I say to you, that you will weep and
lament, but the world will rejoice; you will be sorrowful,
but your sorrow will be turned to joy. (John 16:20)*

If God is going to use circumstances as discipline in our
lives, He will apprise us of their purpose. Everything He
does is by design. Many times such trials, suffering, and
grief-producing situations are tests so that we might be
better prepared for future ministry. After all, God's leaders are always appointed for a *time of affliction* before
they can be used by Him.

Maybe you're saying to yourself, "Good, then let God
call someone else to be a leader because I don't want the
pain!" Many of those He called thought the same thing.
In fact, many of them even related that to God.

Take, for instance, Jonah. "The word of the Lord came
to Jonah the son of Amittai saying, 'Arise, go to Nineveh
the great city, and cry against it, for their wickedness has
come up before Me.' But Jonah rose up to flee to Tarshish
from the presence of the LORD. So he went down to Joppa,
found a ship which was going to Tarshish, paid the fare,
and went down into it to go with them to Tarshish from

the presence of the LORD." (Jonah 1:1-3)

Jonah didn't just express his thoughts, he ran in the opposite direction as fast as he could. But the Lord had a plan that would mold Jonah's desires to His own. "And the LORD hurled a great wind on the sea and there was a great storm on the sea so that the ship was about to break up. Then the sailors became afraid, and every man cried to his god, and they threw the cargo which was in the ship into the sea to lighten *it* for them. But Jonah had gone below into the hold of the ship, lain down, and fallen sound asleep. So the captain approached him and said, 'How is it that you are sleeping? Get up, call on your god. Perhaps *your* god will be concerned about us so that we will not perish.'" (Jonah 1:4-6)

Poor Jonah! First he attempted to flee from God and now the Lord not only found him anyway, but Jonah is about to be discovered by the rest of the men on the boat. Here they're giving him an opportunity to *prove that his God is all powerful* and he can't even claim that publicly because he's in a total state of disobedience. Ever felt like that? When we're in our worst moods or about to head the wrong way, the Lord will either send someone to us or have them call. And as we begin to speak about Him, a sense of conviction will wash over us like those giant waves that were about to sink the boat that Jonah had hoped would save him.

Now what? "Then the men became extremely frightened and they said to him, 'How could you do this?' For the men knew that he was fleeing from the presence of the LORD, because he had told them. So they said to him, 'What should we do to you that the sea may become calm for us?'—for the sea was becoming increasingly stormy. And he said to them, 'Pick me up and throw me into the sea.

Then the sea will become calm for you, for I know that on account of me this great storm *has come* upon you.'" (Jonah 1:10-12)

For a while the men tried frantically to continue rowing but to no avail. *They had come up against a God who involved Himself directly and personally with His creation.* They assumed all bases were covered when they requested that each man pray to his own god. One of these gods would assuredly come through, right? But on this day the *real God*, the only One who could truly tame the sea, would demonstrate His power.

Having exhausted all reasonable solutions, these men began *praying to Jonah's God.* Obviously He had demonstrated more force than their idols so they called on Him for help. Do you handle your own terror and grief this way? Do you tell yourself, "I guess I've tried everything and still there's no solution in sight. I may as well ask God for help!" As you attempt to scale the heights of turmoil, are you slipping on loose rocks and losing your footing fast? Well, so was Jonah.

Finally, the men threw him overboard and the sea stopped raging. Jonah heard those unbelievers pleading with God for help, but at this point he still hadn't requested any assistance for himself. Oh, that guilty conscience gets us every time! First we're disobedient, and then we ignore God as if it were all His fault in the first place. How much grief and misery can Jonah endure before he will shriek out to be rescued?

God is about to turn the burner up a notch by dispatching a great fish to swallow Jonah. Meanwhile, the men on the boat are honoring God, offering a sacrifice, and making vows. That's another tried and true human technique: "Just answer this prayer and I'll do whatever you want,

Lord!" But do we? As soon as He removes us from the pressure cooker, we return to the same despicable condition as before.

However, God has managed to get Jonah's attention, after *three days and three nights* in the stomach of the fish, that is! If you're beginning to consider this a real fish story, listen to what Jesus said about Jonah. "For just as JONAH WAS TREE DAYS AND THREE NIGHTS IN THE BELLY OF THE SEA MONSTER, so shall the Son of Man be three days and three nights in the heart of the earth. The men of Nineveh shall stand up with this generation at the judgment, and shall condemn it because they repented at the preaching of Jonah; and behold, something greater than Jonah is here." (Matthew 12:40)

Jesus demonstrated this *identical power over the elements* when a great storm arose, threatening to capsize the boat in which He and the disciples were together. The disciples' reaction to these high waves was one of pure panic, while Christ maintained complete calmness, to the point of falling asleep in the boat. Unable to withstand this frightful scene any longer, they awoke Him saying, "'Save *us*, Lord; we are perishing!' And He said to them, 'Why are you timid, you men of little faith?' Then He arose, and rebuked the winds and the sea; and it became perfectly calm." (Matthew 8:25, 26) This is the same God on whom Jonah relied to save him, and He is absolutely awesome!

Jesus used the illustration of Jonah as *a comparison to His own death, burial, and Resurrection after three days.* The disciples needed to understand that this would not be the end of the story. Although Jonah didn't actually die, he was certainly as good as dead if God hadn't shown mercy and saved him. That's what Christ's death accomplished for us. We are now saved from spiritual death and separation from God.

Yes, Jonah eventually got his act together and began praying to God concerning his distress. He begged and pleaded when it became abundantly clear that God was neither going to let him drown nor run away. Take some time to read the entire account of Jonah's leadership training. He begins by reminding the Lord of all the good things he's done, reiterating that he doesn't deserve this kind of treatment. After all, Jonah had "looked toward the holy temple!" (Jonah 2:4) In other words, he had shown up at the worship services. Therefore, when requesting assistance he expected God's *immediate response*. Aren't we just the same?

Talk about being turned around, maybe that cool dip in the swirling water affected Jonah's brain. We owe God gratitude for our next breath and every one thereafter. The gifts He chooses to bestow on us during our weakest moments are the undeserved actions of One who deeply loves us.

However, like any loving father, God must *discipline* us if we're going to turn out all right. At times this discipline falls neatly under the heading of *suffering and grief*. Jonah had been selected by God to become a prophet. How could he possibly perform in this capacity if he chose to run every time God called? The Lord taught him a powerful lesson on *submission to the will of God*. God's strong hand of protection could keep him safe despite either the elements of nature or the actions of men.

On the third day God caused the great fish to spew Jonah up onto the seashore. God then called him again, requesting that he proclaim the message to Nineveh. This time Jonah complied. Does this remind you of Peter's own grief-filled account of needing a second chance after having denied Christ? After the Resurrection Jesus returned not only to demonstrate that Peter was forgiven, but also to give him a fresh call back to the ministry of being a "fisher of men."

As a result of Jonah's *obedience,* the city of Nineveh repented, and the people abandoned their wicked and violent ways. However, Jonah's story doesn't end there. Jonah, who had been the recipient of the Lord's mercy and rescue, becomes angry at God for sparing Nineveh from destruction. As a Jew, Jonah desired to deliver the prophecy of impending doom and then watch as God demonstrated his awe-inspiring power over these 120,000 Gentiles. But the Lord worked carefully to instill compassion within Jonah's heart for all people. Like Jonah, through our own grief and agony we are able to learn understanding. *God's discipline* is always administered to *teach a lesson.*

Let's consider the call of Noah. Although the story of Noah is probably familiar, perhaps you haven't considered it as an example of God's training ground or as an account of God's own broken heart in response to sin. "Then the LORD saw that the wickedness of man was great on the earth, and that every intent of the thoughts of his heart was only evil continually. And the LORD was sorry that He had made man on the earth, and He was grieved in His heart. And the LORD said, 'I will blot out man whom I have created from the face of the land, from man to animals to creeping things and to birds of the sky; for I am sorry that I have made them.' But Noah found favor in the eyes of the LORD." (Genesis 6:5-8)

At that point in time, there were only eight people—Noah and his family—who did not deserve to be annihilated from the face of the earth. Consider the full weight of the *grief-filled information* God shares with Noah. All the people he's ever known are going to be drowned in a great flood and it's Noah's job to *obey God's instructions* and construct an ark that will carry his family through this debacle to safety. Noah must *trust God* as never before, working on the ark each day while also *delivering the message.*

The physical task of building such an immense structure as the ark became one consideration. However, *following God* had also rendered Noah a "nut case" to those around him. Noah quickly became initiated into the world of grief in more ways than one. For starters, it had never rained before. (Genesis 2:5, 6) Previously, God sent a mist that arose on the earth and covered the surface of the ground. Now God had decreed a *judgment by flood.*

However, God's mercy prevented this downpour immediately. We know the duration of time from when Noah received the call until God shut the door of the ark to be 120 years. Noah therefore suffered the scorn and derision of these people on a daily basis for over a century! Can't you picture the people walking by, kids in hand, jeering at the human landmark? "And there's old Noah, who's making himself an ark, because he *thinks* there's going to be something called a *flood.*" How devastating for Noah, never winning one soul over to the truth.

Again we can observe the difference in Noah's response from that of Jonah. Noah was "a righteous man, blameless in his time; Noah walked with God." (Genesis 6:9) Certainly being that close to God, he understood the Lord's grief at being rejected by those who chose to forfeit a relationship with Him. We also know that Noah carried out *all that the Lord commanded* and still grief followed. From

Second Peter 2:5 we learn that Noah was a "preacher of righteousness." Noah faithfully continued to deliver God's message despite the ridicule and unbelief that encompassed him like a band of hungry hyenas.

If only the people of Noah's time could have grasped the concept that is presented over and over in the Psalms! "But the salvation of the righteous is from the LORD; He is their strength in time of trouble. And the LORD helps them, and delivers them; He delivers them from the wicked, and saves them, because they take refuge in Him." (Psalm 37:39, 40)

Unlike Nineveh, the population of Noah's world would not redress their sin. When the deluge began, the whirling waters washed them all away. But Noah clung to the Lord's promises, *abiding in His word.* He had passed this comprehensive exam, despite great obstacles, a test that had lasted for over a century and a quarter. *Noah continued to believe God.*

Noah carried with him the deep heartache of knowing that no one else save his family would survive. Mercifully the Lord closed the door of the ark; God Himself watched and allowed this final judgment to stand.

Lest we become tempted to draw a wrong conclusion about the character of God, remember that all of these people were provided ample time to have *listened* and *acted* upon the warning that God delivered through Noah. God's judgments are always just! During another time in history God sent angels to deliver a similar message of pending doom. "Now the men of Sodom were wicked exceedingly and sinners against the LORD." (Genesis 13:13) The degree of punishment matched the depth of debauchery, and only Lot and his daughters were spared from the fiery inferno. (Genesis 19:27-30)

Are you beginning to see a pattern? God punishes disobedience. But the Lord *always* warns men and women when He's about to take action against their offenses. Like Sodom, in which homosexuality was rampant (Genesis 19:4-5), the world today continues to *condone evil* and refuses to repent. God's impending judgment for the final days of the world as we know it promises to be more cataclysmic than all previous disasters. Are we willing to carry the message of Noah and Jonah into a world that *knows Him not*?

Unlike Jonah, who sought to run the other way, Jesus Christ walked right into the middle of issues. But He was also led by the very Spirit of God to speak plainly about the *sources of grief* on earth. Similarly, Paul, the apostle, also warned us: "Now the deeds of the flesh are evident, which are: immorality, impurity, sensuality, idolatry, sorcery, enmities, strife, jealousy, outbursts of anger, disputes, dissensions, factions, envyings, drunkenness, carousing, and things like these, of which I forewarn you just as I have forewarned you that those who practice such things shall not inherit the kingdom of God." (Galatians 5:19-21)

Those who have chosen to believe in Christ are empowered by God to offset the evil in the world and live according to the words of Jesus. "But the fruit of the Spirit is love, joy, peace, patience, kindness, goodness, faithfulness, gentleness, self-control; against such things there is no law. Now those who belong to Christ Jesus have crucified the flesh with its passions and desires. If we live by the Spirit, let us also walk by the Spirit." (Galatians 5:22-25)

In the midst of evil Noah made a difference on the earth, while in another perverse generation, Jonah called men to repentance. How much of our suffering is due to our own disobedience? Each of us must search our own hearts and then come to the foot of the cross with an awareness of our failings. For only Christ, who displayed in unlimited measure every aspect of the character of God, can free us to live an exemplary life in the midst of our own depraved generation.

Once we have *submitted obediently* to His authority, He will call us to bring the Gospel message to others. Every kind of suffering in this world can be traced back to sin, which can only result in suffering and death. In a previous chapter we saw how Adam and Eve's sin brought *death and suffering* into the world. Sin is here to stay and the only way through it is to obtain a *new nature* from Christ. No group of individuals is to blame for the mess this world is in; in the end we've all contributed to its sad state in one way or another.

Therefore, it is paramount that we use the gifts of God's Spirit to reach out to others while we still can. To become lethargic now would be the worst sin of all. Will we model ourselves on Jonah and gladly await the destruction of the wicked? Or will we continue to bring the *Good News* to those living in desperation, as Jesus Christ?

Perhaps you didn't experience *unconditional love* from your parents. Not many people have. With a child come expectations, hopes, and each parent's own dreams. When these aren't met, despair takes up residence in our hearts. But no matter how your human parents might have failed, your Father in heaven hasn't and won't.

However, God also cannot become so overprotective that He never allows us to suffer the consequences of our own actions. If we're really honest we'll admit that some choices we've exercised have brought misery, not only to ourselves but also to others.

This *pain* from our heartache and misery propels us toward God. Had I not tired of my own agony, I would not have become a Christian. That haunting loneliness and isolation drove me to seek Him. Therefore, if God removes our pain, we'll never discover how He desired to assist us through it.

Do you believe that death is the end of everything? If you answered in the affirmative, it's no wonder you're without hope! Have you forgotten that Christ has conquered death? Remember what Jesus said to Martha: "I am the resurrection and the life; he who believes in Me shall live even if he dies, and everyone who lives and believes in Me shall never die. Do you believe this?" (John 11:25, 26) Jesus conquered death and came back to prove that we can experience everlasting life in Him.

Another benefit of pain and sorrow is that it actually enables us to loosen our grip on this earthly life. Imagine what life would be like if our bodies never wore out. Would life in heaven seem so appealing then? Paul, who suffered untold persecution and bodily affliction for the Gospel, understood this. "For this perishable must put on the imperishable, and this mortal must put on immortality." (1 Corinthians 15:53) As we anticipate shedding these worn-out bodies of ours and receiving ones that will not deteriorate, we are letting go of what was and looking forward to what will be with God.

After Jonah searched in vain for an exit sign inside that huge fish, he finally learned to trust God with all his heart. And God came through. *God also has an answer for your own grief and pain.*

God never asks us to go it alone. He's already been there and done that, and Jesus has nail-pierced hands to prove it! You cannot and will not suffer more than Christ: ". . .So His appearance was marred more than any man, And His form more than the sons of men." (Isaiah 52:14) As Christ leaned under the weight of His cross and attempted to walk down the narrow streets of Jerusalem, people actually began weeping at the sight of Him. Jesus had become nearly unrecognizable as a human being. Our suffering here on earth cannot equal that.

Perhaps the greatest disservice is to pretend that each life surrendered to Christ will not contain a measure of suffering. For it surely will. However, the presence of Christ within that life far outweighs anything that might seem of benefit without Him. Did Jonah considered turning back the clock to how things were before he finally cried out to God for help? Never! Being in the belly of that great fish had convinced him that God could keep him safe, despite the most bizarre circumstances. Likewise, all that's sitting back at that distant bend in the road before we chose Christ is the suitcase of emptiness we willingly abandoned. Ahead stretches the road to *eternity*.

Another benefit of suffering is that of compassion for others. Eventually Jonah learned this lesson. In fact, the very reason Jonah cited for running from this assignment in the first place was that he knew God to be "gracious and compassionate. . .slow to anger and abundant in loving kindness, and one who relents concerning calamity." (Jonah 4:2)

Jonah's real concern had been that he would go into this heathen land only to have God forgive these people and relinquish His threat. God's chosen leader had viewed God's forgiveness and yet hadn't allowed this attribute to penetrate his mind and heart.

Instead, Jonah sat under the leafy plant, which God had caused to grow as shade over him, bemoaning that God had observed the repentant hearts of the Ninevites. What did God then do? First, He caused a worm to attack the plant and it withered. ". . .God appointed a scorching east wind, and the sun beat down on Jonah's head so that he became faint and begged with *all* his soul to die. . ." (Jonah 4:8) During the rest of their ensuing conversation, the Lord relates to Jonah that he has no right to be angry concerning God's decisions. Are you also holding onto a point of grief that perhaps stems from an action exercised by God?

As we suffer God will handpick those with sympathetic hearts who can walk in step beside us. Their hugs will envelop us like a blanket of understanding, while their words will manage to smooth out the wrinkles in our tormented and grieving minds. We will know without any doubt that God truly cares.

Only through suffering did Jonah understand. Only God has the power to take our lumpy and shapeless mass of suffering and remold it for our ultimate good. Through pain, agony, and abandonment, God shaped Jonah into a leader He could use. Are you allowing the Lord *free rein* within the sarcophagus of your own grief? Remember, only God can turn your sorrow into joy. "I lift up my eyes to the hills—where does my help come from? My help comes from the LORD, the Maker of heaven and earth." (Psalm 121:1-2, NIV)

11

God's Saddlebags
of Salve

*But I say to you who hear, love your enemies, do good
to those who hate you, bless those who curse you, pray
for those who mistreat you. (Luke 6:27, 28)*

One of the last tasks Jesus performed before His sacrificial death was to forgive those who had placed Him on the cross. He forgave not just the men who stood around firmly clutching hammers in their strong, burly hands, but *all of us*. Jesus left this legacy of mercy as an example for us to live by. As our Creator, He understood full well that harboring bitterness and anger would choke the life out of us quicker than anything else. Yet most humans would gladly undergo dental work without benefit of anesthetic rather than relinquish a fistful of vengeance against those who have harmed them.

The media have embraced what is termed "the recovery movement," and evidence of its popularity can be seen in newsstands, libraries, and Christian bookstores. Admittedly, many have genuinely benefited from their therapeutic flashbacks into the past, acquiring a balance of the bitter with the sweet. But consider those who have chosen to demonstrate their newly adopted insight by learning to blame, accuse, alienate, and even file suit against their abusers! Has liberal use of this freeing liniment rendered us a more peaceful society?

One has only to sit in a weekly Twelve-Step meeting for several months to comprehend that injured parties are attempting to wallow where they once only waded. Before the pendulum of censure swings into uncharted territory, *this wound of awakening* must quickly receive a heretofore unnamed unguent while there's still something worthwhile to salvage. God calls it *forgiveness.*

Our bus has gone way past the street called *Honesty* and we are instead disembarking in a neighborhood called *Disintegration.* But God has a transfer ticket available that will mend those broken relationships. When most of Jesus' apostles abandoned Him at the foot of the cross He forgave them. While callous and vengeful men beat Him unmercifully with lead-laced whips, He refused to retaliate. From the cross He pleaded with the Father to *forgive us,* understanding that we had no concept of real, abiding, sacrificial love until He came. Now we can look back at His cross with the perspective of comprehension.

When my dear friend Emilie Barnes speaks at conferences, she offers a precious commodity at her well-organized book and product table. It's a small white can, about the size of a spice container. Printed on the outside, in either red or blue, is the word LOVE, which Emilie sprinkles liberally both in her home and on those she meets elsewhere.

At the 1994 Southern California Christian Women's Retreat, Emilie's husband Bob held a workshop, "How to Stand by Your Man." First he stated the obvious, that we are all sinners. But then he continued, "Change is a choice which grows more plentifully in an atmosphere of praise."

Bob related that for many years the women in Emilie's Bible studies had prayerfully recorded on small pieces of paper all the improvements they desired for their husbands. These were then folded and placed in a special little box. Throughout the duration of the study they would pray diligently while watching the Lord weave miraculous changes in their husbands. The Lord truly freed these women from anger, frustration, and futility.

Because God has forgiven our sins, we, too, can forgive others and change our habits and outlook. Although the recovery movement did manage to bring suffering and grief into sharper focus, it can't alter the truth. *Our recovery must lead to forgiveness or it's invalid.* Progress is slow but pain remains a good teacher.

Nothing can amend the past, no matter how hard we may wish that something traumatic hadn't occurred. Attempts to inflict anguish on the lives of those who have injured us will not serve to alleviate our torments either. Simply because God's justice appears *slow* in coming doesn't mean it isn't *sure*.

These feelings of helplessness and victimization perpetuate our hatred for those who either knowingly or unknowingly invaded our trust and warped our sense of security. But nothing escapes the view of our omnipotent God and He has promised to make it right. "God judgeth the righteous, and God is angry with the wicked every day." (Psalm 7:11, KJV)

The more you understand the Lord, the easier it is to allow Him to fight your battles. "If a man does not repent, He will sharpen His sword; He has bent His bow and made it ready." (Psalm 7:12) Do you now accept that God cares enough to intervene?

Jesus fostered reconciliation. His life and death proved

that to us. Now He expects us to use His enabling power to restore those who have become estranged from us. In her book *Midwife For Souls*, Kathy Kalina maintains that *"reconciliation* is not a feeling but *an act of the will."** Exercising this important decision can make all the difference in how our loved ones are ushered into the next world. Certainly we should observe ways in which we can resolve issues rather than accelerate ongoing friction.

What better gift could we bestow on those we hold dear than to surround them with the affection of their families? Here's a bitter truth: One minute after a dear one is gone we will recall with graphic clarity *our own life failures*, not theirs. This only multiplies the depth of mounting grief as we begin wishing with all our hearts that we had said or done more to *make things right.*

Every time we refuse to comply with Christ's example of forgiveness we add more weight to our luggage of suffering. Many of the personal accounts contained in this book have served to reinforce this truth. Considering the harmful effects of unresolved issues, we cannot afford to allow these to seep in through an open basement window and permeate every facet of our lives.

Patsy Dooley, a humorist and management specialist from Grover Beach, California, explains to her audiences the ways in which stress invades their daily routine, robbing them of productivity. For instance, many people don't realize the detrimental effects of intense anxiety on our thought processes. Why else would so many of us tease about the early onset of old age? We become fretful, forgetful, and even frightened in our homes and offices. One more crisis will send us completely over the edge, we're sure of it!

*Boston: St. Paul Books & Media, 1993, p. 38.

But what we may not realize is that all this tension and pressure is usurping vital energy that could be used in not only reestablishing relationships, but, more importantly, in spreading the hopeful message of the Gospel. Isn't it just like Satan to involve us in a "battle for our rights?" The focus of such a conflict is then on *self* rather than on *God's power to sustain us.*

Speaking to the Corinthians, Paul reinforced this fact: "For the kingdom of God does not consist in words, but in power." (1 Corinthians 4:20) Paul attempted to teach that *speaking* about the kingdom carried reality to nonbelievers only if they were also willing to *live out* the message Christ left for them. For it is in observing God's transformation within a life that the true power of the Word is demonstrated.

Christ continually reminded the disciples to believe not only *His Word* but also *His works,* which demonstrated God's power. Without this reinforcing combination there is no testimony. Therefore, refusing to absolve those who have injured us tends to negate any proof that we have actually received spiritual renewal from Christ.

Susan Blumenthal, M.D., has written about a "silent epidemic" in the United States caused by the many abused women who never confer with their physicians concerning the incidents. Seeking an end to this suppression of truth, Dr. Blumenthal presented the following startling statistics: "Each day in the U.S., ten women die as the result of domestic violence; every fifteen seconds a woman is beaten; every six minutes a woman is raped."*

Does Christ expect us to pardon even these crimes? Yes, because He forgave those who tormented Him. "Father,

---

*Susan Blumenthal, M.D., "Health Newsletter," *Elle* magazine, October 1994, p. 148.

forgive them; for they do not know what they are doing." (Luke 23:34) This isn't offered as some trite platitude. Jesus actually released this pain and agony to the Father while He hung on the cross. His combination of *words* and *actions* spoke volumes to the man hanging next to Him.

Upon hearing this, this criminal requested, "Jesus, remember me when You come into Your kingdom!" (Luke 23:42) The thief on the cross understood Christ's clear message of salvation and responded in belief. Jesus promised him paradise.

This, then, is the first reason we must *forgive:* Christ gave us His example to follow and will enable us, through His power, to pardon others. Those who know Him as Savior and Lord have already been forgiven by Him.

Speaking of Christ, Paul said, "Of Him all the prophets bear witness that through His name everyone who believes in Him has received forgiveness of sins." (Acts 10:43) In a previous chapter the importance of names within the Middle Eastern culture was discussed. Reflect for a moment on Isaiah's prophecy concerning the Messiah who would come: "Therefore the Lord Himself will give you a sign: Behold, a virgin will be with child and bear a son, and she will call His name Immanuel." (Isaiah 7:14) In Matthew 1:23 we learn that this name, Immanuel, means "God with us." Therefore, it is this very *God with us* who has not only taught us how to forgive, but has also extended forgiveness to us.

Standing below His cross was another who came to believe as a result of hearing His words and observing His actions. "Now when the centurion saw what had happened, he *began* praising God, saying, 'Certainly this man was innocent.'" (Luke 23:47) As he watched as Jesus dismissed His spirit, the centurion knew the truth. Christ had remained in control of the situation, all the while enduring the hellish torment of man. And yet He forgave. The centurion saw Jesus' power of forgiveness in action and therefore believed.

Through this faith in who Jesus is we become ambassadors for Him. "Thus it is written, that the Christ should suffer and rise again from the dead the third day; and that repentance for forgiveness of sins should be proclaimed in His name to all the nations, beginning from Jerusalem." (Luke 24:46, 47) There it is again: His agony without retaliation is the very key to opening up the hearts of those who seek forgiveness. Jesus has chosen each of us to bring this message to our hurting world. But how can we accomplish this purpose if we fail to absolve those who seek our forgiveness?

Sometimes our pain and suffering at the hands of others has been so excruciating that we may feel incapable of ever letting go of tormented memories and graphic flashbacks. This is when we need desperately to trust the inspired words of Paul: "For He delivered us from the domain of darkness, and transferred us to the kingdom of His beloved Son, in whom we have redemption, the forgiveness of sins." (Colossians 1:13, 14) Satan cannot impair us with these memories as God's power is sufficient not only to free us from bondage of the past, but also to recreate *hope* within us. And hope is, after all, the chief desire of our wounded spirits.

When the Israelites pleaded for release from their bondage in Egypt, God saved them by drying up the Red Sea that they might cross safely. "Nevertheless He saved them for the sake of His name, that He might make His power known." (Psalm 106:8, 9) Through the miracle of healing

He will perform in your own body, mind, and spirit, others will understand He truly is our *powerful God.*

That's why it's vitally important that we know the Word of God. As we study the ways in which He has dealt with humankind in the past, we can comprehend not only how awesome He is but also confidently depend on Him for the solutions we require. If you've suffered pain and affliction at the hands of another, you require God's balm of healing, and it comes packaged two ways. First, it's within the pages of His Word, the Bible, where you can learn about His Son. And second, it's housed within those who truly love Him. His Spirit will dispense this balm to you, as needed, because the supply is absolutely unlimited.

What drew men to Christ? The same attributes that attract us to Him today. There is the assurance *you won't be turned away.* As He began His ministry, Jesus sought out those who would serve with Him. The first called were Peter and Andrew, whom He found while walking by the Sea of Galilee. "And He said to them, 'Follow Me, and I will make you fishers of men.'" (Matthew 4:19) We know that they complied immediately. Did they understand the cost? Not then, but they soon would, as noted in previous chapters.

Consider the story of the Samaritan woman who came to a well to draw water. She hadn't come early in the morning when all the other women arrived at the well. Her despicable lifestyle had alienated her from associating with them. But on this particular day she met Jesus, and He changed her life forever. Jesus took the time to explain to her that He was the source of *living water.* She not only believed Him and responded, but she ran to tell everyone she knew. She had never met a man who showed her *such respect,* especially after He had fully comprehended the substance of her life. (John 4:6-28)

In another account, Jesus took pity on a man who grieved over being paralyzed for thirty-eight years. Others had observed this man every day and yet never assisted him to move toward the healing waters of the pool at Bethesda. Jesus asked, "Do you wish to get well?" (John 5:6) When the man responded, He healed him. Not only was this a tremendous miracle, but it was also a great risk. Jesus had healed this man on the Sabbath and this enraged the religious leaders who from then on would seek to kill Him. However, for the sake of those who might respond, Jesus willingly placed Himself in jeopardy.

Christ urgently occupied every moment He spent on earth in order to fulfill God's Word before the eyes of these chosen people. He sought to release those who had been oppressed, enslaved, and dominated by both false religion and other nations. Many times His disciples had to remind Him to take time to eat. His reply refocused their own priorities. "Do you not say, 'There are yet four months, and *then* comes the harvest'? Behold, I say to you, lift up your eyes, and look on the fields, that they are white for harvest." (John 4:35)

Although fully conscious of the urgency of time, Jesus never hurried. Instead, He made Himself available to those who desperately sought physical or spiritual healing, others who required understanding, and still more who had been afflicted or rejected by the world. Is it any wonder that the people flocked to Him?

Statistics abound concerning violence among children and teenagers in our nation. One article stated that between 1970 and 1991, for example, about 50,000 children were killed by guns.* Unbelievable, isn't it?

Perhaps the fact that I grew up in the 1950s explains

---

*"What Our Children Need Is Adults Who Care," *Parade* magazine, October 9, 1994, p. 5.

my culture shock over such information. Each number represents a unique human being who will never walk this earth again, and that is grief!

Two of my own cousins became victims of gun violence. One was approached by a stranger in a restaurant who mistook him for someone else, raised a gun to his head, and shot him to death. Now his lovely wife and precious sons are left to wonder every day why this senseless act took place. He never saw his fortieth birthday.

The pressure and stresses of my other cousin's unresolved life traumas created an unseen cage that began closing in on him. Nothing was divulged to those who loved him and would have intervened. Instead, he took a gun to his head and killed himself. After nearly fifteen years, the pain of his death is still with his family and friends. The "if onlys" we share with one another contain no substance or solace. Our family simply goes on without his unique contributions. Grief has taken up residence with us.

I find myself wishing that every child could have enjoyed the time in America when neighbors cared for one another, sick or well. They talked to one another and shared their concerns as well as joyful tidings. They structured time to worship God in church each week and respected their fellow citizens. Everyone viewed wholesome television shows. A handshake sealed a deal, because a person's word could be relied upon. I find myself *grieving* for this bygone era in which people *trusted one another.* When men and women began *ignoring God* as their Creator, they also *lost all hope* in one another.

Although these times are now history, Jesus Christ hasn't changed. The miracles He wrought within souls can still take place today. He remains faithful, poised, and ready to listen to you, no matter where you hurt or who is responsible for the pain. Are you willing to bring yourself to Him so that He can begin that work of inner healing so desperately required? If we allow Him to instill new life within us, perhaps the grief of this present age can be lessened for our children.

12

A Valise of Variety

For all things are for your sakes, that the grace which is spreading to more and more people may cause the giving of thanks to abound to the glory of God.
(2 Corinthians 4:15)

Within each of our lives there exist wrenching episodes that knock our perspective out of kilter. No one will likely be tempted to consider this present valise of grief a "Kodak moment." During the season in which these incidents occur, we would be hard pressed to acknowledge them as memoirs or keepsakes.

Instead, we devise ways to anesthetize the pain and suffering that have befallen us. We focus instead on denying we were placed on this earth to "walk by faith, not by sight." (2 Corinthians 5:7) What is this human malady that dictates we must *always comprehend immediately*?

When taking a course at a college or university, we initially allow ourselves some time to become acquainted with a subject. However, when it comes to life as a whole, we demand instant recognition and accountability for all manner of maladies. Most often we're also searching for a target at which to hurl our darts of blame and accusation. How easily we draft God to become that bull's-eye!

So, what's the real purpose of suffering, and is there

any hope? "We *are* afflicted in every way, but not crushed; perplexed, but not despairing; persecuted, but not forsaken; struck down, but not destroyed; always carrying about in the body the dying of Jesus, that the life of Jesus also may be manifested in our body." (2 Corinthians 4:8-10) We suffer, then, *that God's glory may be demonstrated* in our lives. For as He rescues and resuscitates our spirits from what might appear to be the brink of desolation, others may view this renewal and learn to rely on Him themselves.

Is there a way to insulate ourselves from such grief and agony? For one thing, we can stop being shocked at its appearance. "Beloved, do not be surprised at the fiery ordeal among you, which comes upon you for your testing, as though some strange thing were happening to you; but to the degree that you share the sufferings of Christ, keep on rejoicing; so that also at the revelation of His glory, you may rejoice with exultation." (1 Peter 4:12, 13) *Being prepared* helps to lessen the initial fear and anxiety. God said trials would come and they do, with regularity.

We can also *stay closely attached to Christ.* Someday the picture of us may resemble Him, in that our essence will have been altered because of this very affliction and misery. He endured all manner of agony for us, that the character and glory of God might shine forth as we *abide* in Christ.

The perspective we seek on pain cannot be viewed apart from Him. But where does *hope* enter the scene? "And not only this, but we also exult in our tribulations, knowing that tribulation brings about perseverance; and perseverance, proven character; and proven character, hope; and hope does not disappoint, because the love of God has been poured out within our hearts through the Holy Spirit who was given to us." (Romans 5:3-5) Does it help to realize that suffering has a purpose?

Now there you have it: The *Spirit of God* not only enables us to understand the reason for trials, tragedy, and travail, but also provides *hope* for our muddled and questioning minds. Think back to David, writer of a majority of the Psalms. In spite of his confusion over the despicable events and circumstances of his life, David penned his honest longings, questions, and doubts to his loving and compassionate God. This provided the impetus for a responsive and relinquished heart, allowing the Lord to renew his spirit.

Perhaps you've read the account of how David took Bathsheba, the wife of Uriah the Hittite, impregnated her, and then had Uriah killed in battle so that he might marry her. Even though David repented, he had been appointed as God's leader, and therefore a beacon of authority to the people. God demanded an accounting. To Nathan, the prophet, fell the task of expressing God's irrevocable pronouncement: "The LORD also has taken away your sin; you shall not die. However, because by this deed you have given occasion to the enemies of the LORD to blaspheme, the child also that is born to you shall surely die." (2 Samuel 12:13, 14)

David and Bathsheba's child did indeed become sick and for seven days David fasted and prayed, begging God to spare the child's life. However, the Lord's Word stood and the child succumbed. David had done all he could and yet the offspring he loved and wanted died. Did he become angry at God? No, because nothing could change God's righteous decision. Therefore David accepted it, comforted his wife, and got on with his life. He had learned a great lesson about obedience to God's commandments as well as the Lord's stringent leadership requirements.

David had also lived out what we know today as the Serenity Prayer: "God grant me the serenity to accept the things I cannot change, the courage to change the things I can and the wisdom to know the difference."* When we've done all we can, it's time to let go and allow God to be God. To do otherwise is to heap further grief, suffering, and misery upon ourselves.

While we're in the Old Testament, let's take a moment to observe Job's attitude toward calamity. Poor old Job endured losing his children, his home, and his flocks. Then his health failed as his body became covered in horrible boils. About this time his wife encourages him to "curse God and die!" (Job 2:9)

However, Job's acceptance of God's rulership didn't hinge on his obtaining all that his heart desired. Instead Job understood the magnificence of his Lord. This attitude is displayed in Job's response to his wife. "But he said to her, 'You speak as one of the foolish women speaks. Shall we indeed accept good from God and not accept adversity?'" (Job 2:10)

As demonstrated in both accounts, David and Job relinquished their lives into the care of God who knew better than either of them what would be required for them to become the people He had designed them to be. Is your concept of God limited simply to all He can give you? What would your reaction be if He chose to take something away?

Switching gears to the New Testament, Paul penned an encouraging letter to Timothy from a prison cell. "Therefore do not be ashamed of the testimony of our Lord, or of

---

*Author unknown.

me His prisoner; but join with *me* in suffering for the gospel according to the power of God, who has saved us, and called us with a holy calling, not according to our works, but according to His own purpose and grace which was granted us in Christ Jesus from all eternity." (2 Timothy 1:8, 9)

Paul relates nothing of his suffering. In fact, he observes this prison experience as confirmation that *Christ has called him into service*. He also sees his trial as *an opportunity to identify with Christ*. Additionally, Paul knows that these circumstances somehow fit into God's grand and unique scheme for his life.

James held what many might call a radical view of detrimental circumstances. "Consider it all joy, my brethren, when you encounter various trials, knowing that the testing of your faith produces endurance. And let endurance have its perfect result, that you may be perfect and complete, lacking in nothing." (James 1:2-4)

Okay, let's get real! How can we possibly hope to be joyful in the midst of sorrow? What James is speaking about isn't happiness, which usually depends on circumstances. Instead, he's addressing the issue of a condition of the heart that has everything to do with *who God is*, regardless of the storms raging all around. James is relating that in the midst of the trial he is not alone. The Lord is there!

Consider that trials and grief came to James and other followers of Christ because they dared to live as Jesus Christ. They dared to be unique in a world that was indifferent to both sin and the God who had become man in order to reach their hearts. The Holy Spirit inspired Paul to record, "And indeed, all who desire to live godly in Christ Jesus will be persecuted." (2 Timothy 3:12) It's a normal outcome of abiding. Just as nurtured and watered apple trees grow delicious fruit, it's predictable.

Why do we spend so much time running from the inevitable? To give a simple answer, we abhor pain. We must, however, be certain that this suffering isn't the result of our own sin. It's one thing to be reviled for our profession of faith, and quite another for sin to be the underlying source of this distress. "For what credit is there if, when you sin and are harshly treated, you endure it with patience? But if when you do what is right and suffer *for it* you patiently endure it, this *finds* favor with God. For you have been called for this purpose, since Christ also suffered for you, leaving an example for you to follow in His steps." (1 Peter 2:20, 21)

There are those who attempt to fill the church with large numbers of "believers" by presenting a gospel that appears to require merely a verbal response. In so doing, they encourage people to "come to Jesus and He'll fix everything in your life, give you the things you want, and make life wonderful!"

Many who respond to Christ as adults have a history of sin and disobedience that in turn are weighted by a suitcase of repercussions. God cannot dispense with either the law of gravity or the laws of thermodynamics to extricate us from a wave of problems we have already set in motion. Each of us must surrender our useless weapons at the foot of the cross, like soldiers in defeat, admitting our sins and then obtaining forgiveness from Christ.

He can and will display a process for turning these mine fields into manageable obstacle courses. Consider a person who finally became a Christian after their drug addiction or alcoholism triggered the loss of a wife or husband, as well as children. The mere fact that they have now entered into a rehabilitation program doesn't automatically mean that their mate will drop the divorce proceedings against them. If substance abuse and the physical harm of loved ones have already taken place, there's no guarantee that these relationships will ever be restored. Mistreatment prevents loved ones from rushing back into a potentially dangerous and desperate situation.

The way back to stability may appear treacherous, but when we call upon the Lord He will uphold us, instilling all of the positive input necessary to get us back on track. Pray for those who have received harm and begin to make amends. Somewhere along their trolley line a glitch in the current, called failure to understand responsibility, has occurred.

Unfortunately, there are times when those we have injured are incapable of viewing our lives from the aspect of renewal. That's when the Twelve-Step phrase, "let go and let God," comes into play. Only God can change a heart, but don't give up trying to reach them.

Another pothole on the road to stability is *anxiety*. Those in recovery experience many distressing and frightening moments of growth. If you're in the throes of such an experience, allow your mind to dwell on the soothing consolation of Christ's own words: "And which of you by being anxious can add a *single* cubit to his life's span? . . .Do not be anxious then, saying, 'What shall we eat?' or 'What shall we drink?' or 'With what shall we clothe ourselves?' For all these things the Gentiles eagerly seek; for your heavenly Father knows that you need all these things." (Matthew 6:27, 31, 32)

God comprehends your necessities better than you. Maybe that's hard to believe, especially if you grew up in a home where your family might have failed you in this regard. But once we've taken the initiative and responded to God's call of commitment, we become qualified for membership in His family. Life then takes on a fresh appearance. So, stop looking backward and begin *anticipating the road ahead.* Remember, God's path will never cause the same desperation as the one you've traveled, because on your new journey Jesus Christ walks the road with you.

Never forget that when Christ restored Peter to fellowship He first took him back in time to the place where he had fallen into sin. Jesus then allowed Peter to reconsider that instance when he had been warned to *pray that he might not fall into temptation.* Peter had to ponder this critical mistake so that he could understand how he arrived there. We, too, must *linger* at that position of despair to experience recovery. Christ then welcomed Peter back into the fold, just as He's also prepared to receive us when we repent.

Since Paul had been the recipient of God's mercy, and his reply to the Lord was one of true contrition, he was more than qualified to encourage the Corinthians. "For just as the sufferings of Christ are ours in abundance, so also our comfort is abundant through Christ. But if we are afflicted, it is for your comfort and salvation; or if we are comforted, it is for your comfort, which is effective in the patient enduring of the same sufferings which we also suffer; and our hope for you is firmly grounded, knowing that as you are sharers of our sufferings, so also you are *sharers* of our comfort." (2 Corinthians 1:5-7)

For the sake of the Gospel Paul had received thirty-nine lashes on five separate occasions, been beaten with rods, stoned, shipwrecked for a night and a day, in peril from robbers as he traveled, and imprisoned. (2 Corinthians 11:24-26) Yet he persevered in bringing the words of hope to those who required them. No grief-causing episode compares to the bleak, despairing condition of life before knowing Christ as Savior. Is your own security in Christ?

Before John, the Gospel writer, died on the island of Patmos, he wrote an inspired final message to the church as well as an account of the final days of the world. Contained in this book of Revelation is an admonition to the church at Ephesus: "But I have this against you, that you have left your first love." (Revelation 2:4)

This warning extends not only to the church but to each of us. Our *first love* must be Jesus Christ. The only way we can manage to support that heavy trunk of *grief and suffering*, which life will present to us "special delivery," is through our identity with Christ. Consider the description of creation from Genesis: "And God created man in His own image, in the image of God He created him; male and female He created them." (Genesis 1:27)

Those who say they are atheists have not only made a purposeful decision to reject the truth, but have also severed the cord of assistance for coping with grief. For who knows how to mend our broken hearts better than our Creator?

Do you remember the covenant God made with Israel? "I will put My law within them, and on their heart I will write it; and I will be their God, and they shall be My people. And they shall not teach again, each man his neighbor and each man his brother, saying, 'Know the LORD,' for they shall all know Me, from the least of them to the greatest of them, declares the LORD, for I will forgive their iniquity, and their sin I will remember no more." (Jeremiah 31:33, 34) This promise stands for all who believe today as well as a future fulfillment for the nation of Israel as a whole. The nation of Israel will ultimately look on the One they pierced and rejected.

The Irish are noted for their sense of humor and through their love of stories and witticisms they bequeath this legacy to their children. My father was no exception. One of his stories concerned a man who was so destitute that he would stand outside a restaurant and *lick the steam off the window*. How aptly this portrays a life without Christ! Although we can enjoy the view through a windowpane, we'll never be able to partake of all that's going on inside. Until we allow Christ the freedom to *work in our hearts*, by having a vital and ongoing relationship with Him, there's no way to heal our grief.

As we remain critically concerned about our own family members, so God stands attentive to our heartaches. "But when the fulness of the time came, God sent forth His Son, born of a woman, born under the Law, in order that He might redeem those who were under the Law, that we might receive the adoption as sons. And because you are sons, God has sent forth the Spirit of His Son into our hearts, crying 'Abba! Father!'" (Galatians 4:4-6)

Isn't that where you ran as a child, to your parent for protection? Jesus has made it possible to return there now, as we pray to our Father, allowing all that anguish, affliction, sorrow, and mourning to flow out in conversation with Him. Go ahead, unload. He can take it!

Believe now that the Lord and His help are real. "The fool has said in his heart, 'There is no God.'" (Psalm 14:1) Throughout your life span, Satan will attempt to convince you that there is no God to alleviate our sense of accountability. Those who assist the evil one in promoting this heinous lie also insist they can't detect when life begins.

Although our lawmakers cannot arrive at the truth, our Creator has already answered this dilemma.

"For Thou didst form my inward parts;
Thou didst weave me in my mother's womb.
I will give thanks to Thee,
for I am fearfully and wonderfully made;
Wonderful are Thy works,
And my soul knows it very well.
My frame was not hidden from Thee,
When I was made in secret,
And skillfully wrought in the depths of the earth.
Thine eyes have seen my unformed substance;
And in Thy book they were all written,
The days that were ordained *for me*,
When as yet there was not one of them.
How precious also are Thy thoughts to me,
O God!
How vast is the sum of them!
If I should count them, they would outnumber
the sand.
When I awake, I am still with Thee." (Psalm
139:13-18)

How can we possibly miss the point here? God says He *planned us, knew us, formed us, and ordained the number of our days on earth.* Life is so very precious to God and He desires that it be cherished by His creation. Perhaps your own grief can become the springboard that will propel you into some life-saving ministry. Certainly there are a number of groups that could benefit from your services. What better way to move forward in your own recovery than to assist others in a cause that promotes what God Himself holds sacred?

Let us ponder again a few of the most critical aspects of grief. First, grief is common to all of us. There are definite stages of grief that we must allow ourselves time to grow through. However, it's impossible to grieve at one time for all the tragic incidents of our lifetime. Instead, each one requires a specific time period.

Remember to be patient with those who are mourning over the loss of loved ones. The process takes an individual amount of healing. Reach out to those who are suffering, either by phone, through cards and letters, or by personal visits. Concentrate on what your friend or loved one requires and not on how you are affected by this loss. As you assist in their grieving process, you'll receive more direction for your own. If your own words seem inadequate, copy a favorite Scripture and send it to them. God promises that His word will never go away.

For children who have lost parents, the key word is *honesty*. Don't make up fairy tale platitudes that may haunt them for the rest of their lives. Answer their questions and encourage them to cry and release the well of grief within them. Little bodies and minds require the same relief from pain as mature ones. How young people learn to handle this sorrowful incident will remain with them forever as a behavior model. This is an excellent time for adults to teach them about God's love and care.

Perhaps the suitcase analogy can encourage you to become aware of and also release your own grief, whether it was mentioned specifically in this book or not. When you become oppressed by the suffering common to each of us, remember most of all how very much the Father loves you. My unrelenting prayer is that you might discover a greater love for Jesus and a deeper understanding of His sacrifice in your behalf. May your example thereby cause a rippling effect of love and compassion directed at others in need. God bless you.

Bibliography

Books and Tapes on Grief and Related issues:

Arthur, Kay. "My Story," Kay Arthur's Testimony of a Wasted Life (cassette tape). Precepts Ministries, P.O. Box 182218, Chattanooga, TN 37422-7218.

Dravecky, Dave and Jan with Ken Gleve. *When You Can't Come Back.* Grand Rapids, MI and San Francisco: Zondervan Publishing House and Harper Collins Publishers, 1992.

Graham, Billy. *Answers to Life's Problems.* Irving, TX: Word, Inc., Publishing, 1960.

————. *Facing Death and the Life After,* A Talking Book, read by Tom Dooley. Available through Billy Graham Evangelistic Association, P.O. Box 779, Minneapolis, MN 55440-0779, Word, Inc., Publishing, 1987.

Heavilin, Marilyn Willett. *Roses in December.* San Bernardino, CA: Here's Life Publishers, Inc., 1986.

————. *Rosas En Invierno (Spanish translation).* Deerfield, FL: Editorial Vida, 1993.

James, Diana L. "What Do We Tell The Children?" (Helping Children Cope With Loss) (cassette tape). Write author at 86-P Calle Aragon, Laguna Hills, CA 92653.

Johnson, A. Wetherell. *Created for Commitment.* Carol Stream, IL: Tyndale House Publishers, 1982.

Kalina, Kathy. *Midwife for Souls*. Boston: St. Paul Books & Media, 1993.

McGinnis, Rev. Jack. "Recovering From Grief," Steps '92 Tape. The Meadows, Whittenburg, PO Box 637, Wickenburg, AZ 85358.

Sanders, J. Oswald. *Heaven, Better By Far*. Discovery House Publishers (also available through Billy Graham Evangelistic Assoc., Minneapolis, MN 55440-0779), 1993.

Smith, Harold Ivan. *Once in a Lifetime: Reflections Upon the Death of a Father*. Nashville: Thomas Nelson Publishers, 1989.

Tangvald, Christine Harder. *Someone I Love Died*. Elgin, IL: Chariot Books, David C. Cook Publishing Co., 1988.

Westberg, Granger E. *Good Grief*. Philadelphia: Fortress Press, 1962.

Books on Christ's Suffering

Lucado, Max. *Six Hours One Friday*. Portland, OR: Multnomah Publishing, 1989.

Books on Prayer and Knowing God

Barnes, Emilie. *15 Minutes Alone with God*. Eugene, OR: Harvest House Publishers, 1994.

Hall, Robert, ed. *The Power of Prayer in a Believer's Life*. Lynwood, WA: Emerald Books, 1993.

Heavilin, Marilyn Willett. *I'm Listening, Lord, Hearing God's Voice When You Pray*. [A fill-in Bible study] Nashville: Thomas Nelson Publishers, 1993.

Pratt, Richard L., Jr. *Pray With Your Eyes Open.* Phillipsburg, NJ: Presbyterian and Reformed Publishing Company, 1987.

Tozer, A. W. *Knowledge of the Holy.* New York: Harper & Row Publishers, Inc., 1961.

Wagner, Peter. *Prayer Shield.* Ventura, CA: Gospel Light Publishers, 1992.

Wirt, Sherwood Eliot. *Jesus Man of Joy.* Nashville: Thomas Nelson Publishers, 1991.

Understanding the Source of our Grief

Alcoholics Anonymous, (Big Blue Book). New York: Alcoholics Anonymous World Services, Inc., 1939.

Hughes, Robert Don. *Satan's Whispers, Breaking the Lies that Bind.* Nashville: Broadman Press, 1992.

Lewis, C. S. *The Screwtape Letters.* New York: Collier Books, Macmillan Publishing Company, 1961.

Littauer, Fred and Florence. *Get A Life Without the Strife.* Nashville: Thomas Nelson Publishers, 1993.

Angels

Rhodes, Ron. *Angels Among Us, Separating Truth From Fiction.* Eugene, OR: Harvest House Publishers, 1994.

ISBN 1-55748-645-X

90000

9 781557 486455